LIVING WITHIN THE SILVER LINING

finding your blessings inside the storms

Living Within The Silver Lining
finding your blessings inside the storms

Ist edition: Copyright © 2009 by Lisa Washington

All right reserved. No part of this book may be reproduced by any mechanical, photographic, or electronic process, or in the form of a phonographic recording; nor may it be stored in a retrieval system, transmitted, or otherwise be copied for public or private use-other than for "fair use" as brief quotations embodied in articles and reviews- without prior written permission of the author.

The author of this book does not dispense medical advice or prescribe the use of any technique as a form of treatment for physical, emotional, or medical problems without the advice of a physician, either directly or indirectly. The material in this book is only for information of a general nature to help inspire you to spiritual well being and health. In the event you use any of the information in this book for yourself, which is your constitutional right, the author and the publisher assume no responsibility for your actions.

ISBN 978-0-557-09078-5

Table of Contents

Introduction……………………………………………………………...	9
Lesson 1~ Learning to be still……………………………………	12
Lesson 2~ Be Authentic……………………………………….…..	16
Lesson 3~ We are all full of faith…………………………………….	19
Lesson 4~ Live in the seasons of life……………………………….	23
Lesson 5~ Friendships in the dark clouds……………………….	26
Lesson 6~ Truth is in love…………………………………………….	29
Lesson 7~ What is your greatest possession?…………………..	32
Lesson 8~ Live in faith not your fears……………………………..	35
Lesson 9~ A short lesson on beauty……………………………….	38
Lesson 10~ The purpose of the physical……………………….	40
Lesson 11~ Getting through the walls…………………………….	43
Lesson 12~ Who is God in my life?...	46
Lesson 13~ The power of your thoughts…………………………..	49
Lesson 14~ Worthy versus Deserving……………………………...	52
Lesson 15~ Come Inside…………………………………. ………..	56
Lesson 16~ Dialysis-a lesson of life………………………………..	59
Lesson 17~ Forgiveness…………………………………………….	62
Lesson 18~ Blessing others from the silver lining…………………	65
Lesson 19~ Let your being be your service – Just be……………..	69
Lesson 20~ Keep your heart open to life…………………………	72
Lesson 21~ You are the message…………………………………….	76
Lesson 22~ Presence versus perfection……………………………..	79
Lesson 23~ Even in the storms we are blessed…………………….	82
Lesson 24~ I am able, because He made it so……………………..	85
Lesson 25~ Find balance within the space life provides………………	88
Lesson 26~ Life is in balance……………………………………….	91
Lesson 27~ It is good to be here………………………………….	95
Lesson 28~ Write your story – Now?..	98
Lesson 29~ Wear your diamonds every day………………………..	102
Lesson 30~ Always go back when you can…………………………	105
Lesson 31~ I am Enough…………………………………………….	107
Lesson 32~ Do what you need to do……………………………….	110
Lesson 33~ Sometimes you can see the rainbow during the storm………	113
Lesson 34~ Who are you making agreements with?...........................	116
Lesson 35~ Your silver lining is always there……………………..	119

Author's Bio.. 121
References.. 122
Resources.. 123

To the joys of my life and
the inspirations of my spirit,
I dedicate this book to my soul mate, my husband Joseph,
and to my two sons, Julian and Tyler

Forward

By Dr. Julie Lord

Lisa is a woman way beyond her years in knowledge, insight and intuition. Anyone needing insight, inspiration, or direction should read this book. Lisa has lived, experienced and suffered more in life than most with kidney disease and many personal tragedies. She has triumphed and found the silver lining over and over again. She is an icon for living in truth and living authentically. Letting go and letting God's spirit move her is a way of life for her. Most of us have one lesson and one gift to give to this world. I am sure you will see Lisa has a gift for everyone and it always comes with a silver lining.

Gratitude List

Julie Lord, thank you for writing my forward and taking care of me in those private moments of life. You are truly a friend and sister.

Nancy Berry, my Editor and friend. Thank you for taking time out to inspire me and make my dreams come true. I have known you for 18 years and you have always made me feel believed in.

Audrey Beauford, my event coordinator for my book launch party, also my best friend of 23 years. You are amazing and I am grateful for our long lasting friendship.

Tami Goodwin, my friend and fabulous event coordinator and owner of StudioID, my go to lady who makes any event I do amazing.

Jennifer Acosta, my Photographer and friend, thank you so much for making me feel beautiful and bringing out the essence of my story in your photos. You are amazing.

The DaVita Dialysis Center staff, thank you guys for making me feel taken care of and making a very challenging time in my life a little bit easier. Your kindness and your hearts moved me so much. God could have not put me in a more perfect center. Continue to touch people's lives with your sincerity and compassion. **You are making a difference.**

The Emory University Hospital staff, thank you for your continued care, your amazing knowledge and compassion for your patients. Thank you Dr. Larsen for being the most amazing surgeon. God has blessed your hands and your heart. You were more than just my surgeon. You made me feel secure and heard throughout this whole process.

The Atlanta Church of Christ in Gwinnett and surrounding churches, thank you for all your prayers and the ways you have served my family over the years. It is because of your prayers we have experienced such an amazing miracle in our lives.

All my friends (you know who you are), thank you for supporting me in all my endeavors, and thank you for encouraging me to write this book. I am grateful for all of you and how each one of you strengthens me and build me up in love. Thanks for your loyalty and being in my corner.

Tracey Kemp, my sister, thank you for being my number one cheerleader. In your eyes and in your laugh, mom is always here with us. I am grateful to God for you. Being with you brings me back and no one makes me laugh like you do. I love you.

Betty Kemp, my mother, though you are not with me in physical form, you are always here, cheering me on. It is your spirit that moves me to creativity and the beauty that surrounds me each day.

To the love of my life Joseph, my love, my friend, my soul mate. Thank you so much for being my knight in shining armor, for coming and rescuing not only my heart, but my life as well. Thank you for allowing God to use you to give me life again, so we can see our dreams come true together.

To my God, thank you for life, and thank you for your unconditional love and compassion. Thank you for moving me each moment of the day. Thank you for giving me the heart to embrace life like never before.

Introduction

As I sit here at my desk and start to write the introduction for this book, my eyes fill with tears and my heart feels a little heavy. I am seeing my life before me, all the things I have faced over the past 20 years. Thoughts run through my mind while I communicate what my soul and spirit have journeyed through over these two decades. I ask myself, will these things I share change someone's life? Will my soul's journey through the dark clouds of life move someone's spirit to be able to reach out for truth, life, and God? But I take another deep breath and my spirit tells me, "Don't worry, the impact of this book will touch the hearts and souls that it must, in the way that it must. You just share your journey." And with that, I pour out to you my heart and some of what has been given to me within the silver lining.

We all are very familiar with the saying, "Every cloud has a silver lining." When we hear this famous phrase, it is usually when we or someone we know is going through a dark cloud in life. It is our way of looking at the bright side of a difficult situation. I have heard this phrase many times in my life. The first time I heard this, I think I was a little girl, and maybe it was my mom who told me to look at my challenges in this way. So as a child I took it to heart and started trying to search for the silver lining in situations, as if I were on some big treasure hunt. I would tell myself, "Lisa, look for the good in this." The advantage of this thinking is that it kept me optimistic. I always thought that in all circumstances the good would eventually show up. The disadvantage was that when I had to persevere through some tough things longer than I felt I needed, I got upset and faithless. I lost all hope and grew depressed about how life was turning out.

I remember growing up in Atlanta with my parents and siblings, always feeling like I was different. I always felt God had something He wanted me to do. I felt I was born for a reason, a very special reason. When I was about eight years old, I wanted to travel to India and wear pretty saris and pray with the monks. When I was ten years old, I told my mom I wanted to join the Peace Corps; she thought I was crazy. When I was 17, I told my mom I was going to become a nun, and yes, she thought I was losing my mind. I just knew I was meant to do something that would bring light and love to the world. I believed I was meant to inspire people to love life. Yes, this may sound like really deep thoughts for a kid, but I felt these things passionately inside. I knew that my life would be a spiritual experience. I believe then and I believe now that life is a spiritual experience.

When I became a teenager, I wanted what the world had to offer. The dream God put in my heart was not cool anymore. Actually people, even in my own family, thought I was a little different to have such ideas. The world and its message were louder than the truth God had placed in me. I got into all kinds of trouble, experimenting with drugs and alcohol, dropping out of school.

Deep inside all I wanted was to be close to God. I remember crying out to God because I felt so far away from what was authentic and true. God heard my prayers and brought into my life some amazing people that shared His love and grace with me. I became a Christian and devoted my life to following Jesus and to sharing His amazing love with others. I felt at this time in my life that I was doing what I was born to do. I was ready to share this new-found faith with others. But God always has more in store for us.

God uses some of our most challenging times to help us bring so much light into the world, even when things seem very dark. Some of my greatest blessings have been within the dark clouds, because God has let me live freely within the silver linings of trials, challenges, loss, chronic illness and many other difficulties. Much of what you are about to read is an accumulation of emails and lessons I sent to friends and family when I was undergoing some very difficult times in my life. In my darkness God showed me the silver lining. I believe that dark clouds will come in every life, but God places a silver lining in each cloud. What do I think is the silver lining? The silver lining is our blessing amongst the trials. I also believe that a silver lining really does lie in *every* dark cloud. Just thinking about this puts butterflies in my tummy, just as it did when I was a child. It is as if I am on a treasure hunt all over again. The question is not *if* there are silver linings in the dark clouds. No, the question is whether I will persevere and stay faithful to find them.

Suggestion for reading:
Take one lesson a day and read and meditate on it. Take one statement that moves you and make it your daily affirmation. I leave you with this blessing:

May you be blessed; may you find what God has placed in you already. May your heart long for truth, and may you drink from His hand and your thirst be quenched. Amen.

~Live Within the Silver Lining~

Stillness is where truth resides.

Lesson 1

Learning to be still

Sometimes it is very easy to forget where we are going or even where we have come from. Why does this happen? Maybe it is because we are always going from one place to the next, from one relationship to the next, from one craze, trend or fad to the next. We go on to a better job, a better house, a better car, a better whatever, always looking on to the next better thing. We accumulate so much in this life, but do we evaluate any of it?

The evaluation doesn't begin with people, things, goals and our greatest dreams. The evaluation process should start with me. I need to take time out, get quiet and be still. I need to listen, observe and embrace, without actions. One of the greatest lessons that I have learned in my life is to be still. I am still exploring this wonderful gift from God. I believe truth can only come when we quiet down the chaos of life. There are so many scriptures in the Bible where God is teaching man to trust Him and let Him be God. **Psalms 46:10 ~ "Be still, and know that I am God."** But sometimes in life God will use the very essence of living to make us be still, and many times I have missed my cue and kept going when I should have been still.

In our fast-paced Western world it is hard to just be still. Some may accuse us of not taking the bull by the horns. There is a time for action, and if we embrace the practice of stillness it will open our hearts at the right time to act.

I remember my first experience with stillness and the lesson it taught me. I was about five years old and my great-aunt was babysitting me one afternoon, when I decided to climb this big tree in her backyard. It was my dream to climb that tree, and today was my day. When I was halfway up, my foot slipped, and as I slid down the tree I scraped my elbow so badly it started to bleed. Once I saw the blood I jumped out the tree and ran inside crying my head off.

My great-aunt ran to my aid immediately. Blood was dripping all down my arm onto the kitchen floor. I just knew my arm was going to fall off, but my aunt took me quietly in her lap and told me, "Now, baby girl, it is going to be all right. I know it hurts right now, but it is going to be all right. Shhh, there, child. Auntie is going to make it all better." I recall my tears slowing as I watched her wash my elbow and kiss my bruise. I believed that I would be all right and she would make it all better.

I became still and allowed myself to be taken care of. She put a band-aid on my elbow and kissed me so many times my face was wet not with tears but with kisses, and she sent me back outside to play.

When I went back out, I was a little more cautious about that tree, but I climbed it again with my elbow still throbbing from the scrape. My mind did not go back to the pain of my elbow; no, my mind went back to that still moment when my aunt calmed me down, quieted my little spirit, and told me I would be all right and took care of me. This is what helped me climb the tree. Now you may think that is not a big deal, but for me at five years old that was a dark cloud. The silver lining was my aunt's comfort and the lesson I learned about being still. She taught me that when life brings hardships, I need to be still and allow myself to be taken care of by God's loving hand.

That is what I need to take with me when it is time for me to act and go back out there and live. It is that time of stillness. My heart and spirit need to remember. I am grateful for the lesson of stillness my great-aunt taught me.

But how do I know when I need to be still? There is a divine plan and our lives are orchestrated by a powerful conductor who looks at all the greatest and smallest details. Only when we are practicing stillness can we recognize that truth. I had to go through some very hard times in my life before I learned to embrace this practice, but it has brought me to a place of peace and serenity no matter what storms I go through. It has made a safe haven for me, a place to return to when I forget how wonderful God is and that He is in control of my life and this amazing journey I face each day. It helps me to remember where I came from and where I am going, and most importantly it helps me to see where I am in my life right now.

Take time out each day and allow yourself to be still.
Meditation:

Turn off the phones, get comfortable, lie down on a blanket or mat.
Make sure you are comfortable and warm.

Inhale as you count to four.
Exhale as you count to five.
Relax each part of your body.
Allow your body to sink deeper into the floor.
Continue to inhale and exhale for at least two to three minutes.
Once the mind is quiet, continue this meditation by just focusing on breathing naturally for five minutes.

When you are ready, roll over to the left side and come to a seated position, placing your hands over your heart.
Take a deep breath and gently open your eyes.

Start your time of prayer, asking, "God, what is it you want me to know?" You may get your answer now, or it may come to you later; just be patient and allow God to give you what is needed when it is needed, no matter what is bothering you.

Authenticity is beyond status. It only answers to Spirit.

Lesson 2

Be authentic

What does it mean to be authentic? Well, here is the dictionary definition: **Authentic** - not false or copied; genuine; real.

Facing life's challenges can put anyone on the defensive. When we feel unhappy and insecure, and life is not going the way we would like it to, pride (ego) is just around the corner. The definition for ego is an exaggerated sense of self-importance and a feeling of superiority to other people. We tend to put on the happy mask to cover up the truth that lives inside of us. When I am not authentic, it affects everything and everyone around me. I believe we have two entities inside of us, the *authentic self* and the *ego self*. The authentic self is our true identity. I believe that is who God designed us to be and who God is trying to create inside of us each and every day. The authentic self lives in truth and not falsehoods. The ego lives in pride, insecurities and lies. It is so much easier to live in our egos. I find myself fighting to not live in the ego. Living in the ego or pride can destroy some of the most beautiful moments in life.

The hardships in life can test who we really are inside, and call us back to what is authentic. I remember when I lost my first baby through a miscarriage. I was so upset with life and with God. I felt betrayed and for a while my battle was trying to get over this pain and get on with life, but that was not being authentic. I thought I was ready to move on. Then it came to me, "What is moving on for me?" When we are being authentic, we ask ourselves such questions; instead of wondering what everyone else is doing and thinking.

This practice of staying connected to my authentic self challenged me even more when I had my second miscarriage. I was 34 years old and my health was getting worse. I was going into my second trimester when I found out the baby's heartbeat had stopped. I was devastated. I knew that I was not going to have babies from my body ever again, that it would not be safe for my health. I felt the same devastation and grief with this miscarriage as I did with the first, but I moved on in a different way. During this time my friend Kimberly Gibson, who knew I loved writing to God, gave me a beautiful journal embroidered in gold. I told her I could not write anything in that journal; she looked at me with her beautiful smile lighting her entire face and said, "Whenever you are ready." I thanked her for the beautiful gift and the kind words. As we stood in my dining room, I told her that God had taught me a great lesson over the years:

"I cannot ride on anyone else's train, because it is not going my way." I believe this is being authentic. We each have our own journey, and for so many years of my life I found myself on the wrong train. Our trains' maybe going in different directions and at different speeds, but only one thing matters, is God, the Great Divine your conductor.

I remember finally writing in the journal that Kimberly gave me. Here is what I wrote:

November 1, 2004
I am sad. I am depressed. I am hurt. I am angry. I feel like a failure. I feel so empty inside. I do not know what to say or what to do. That's all.

I wrote this in my journal a week after I had the miscarriage. I believe, in order to be authentic and not be ruled by your ego (pride), you must stay connected to your Source (God). It doesn't matter how you are connected, whether it is through hours spent praying, reading, or just writing a few sentences in a journal. What matters is that you are connected. When we lose that connection or we refuse to draw near to our Source, we are easily led by ego, and we are pulled to and fro. When the dark cloud of loss came over my life, the lesson from the silver lining was to be authentic in every moment. I had to ask this question to myself, "What does this mean for me?" Being authentic in each moment requires you to be still, turning off the chaos of life and connecting with Spirit, connecting with God.

Fill your faith with good things.

Lesson 3

We are all full of faith

Mark 9:29 says, **"According to your faith will it be done to you."**

You are a very faithful person and your faith has manifested many things in your life. Everyone is faithful. You can look at this statement and say, "No, that is not true. I know a lot of faithless people." However, faith starts with a thought and it moves from there.

The definition for faith in the Bible is found in **Hebrews 11:1, "Now faith is being sure of what we hope for and certain of what we do not see."** Here is another definition: To hope is to believe, desire, or trust.

Sometimes the things we believe desire or trust in are not always positive. Sometimes they are negative and this is what is manifested in our lives. If you are sure that things in your life are never going to change, well, this is your faith about the matter and so it shall be. Sometimes we are so certain of things not changing that things do not change, we do not change. If the blind man's faith was that he could not see, or that Jesus could not restore his sight, than that is exactly what would have happened. God is waiting for us to get faith that says YES to the good in life, but He also responds to the NO, and things in our lives may never change. What you believe is what you will receive.

You can see God in all things because God is the creator of all things. Yoga has taught me about the power of intention, and the need to practice that power every day. I feel the world gives the word "intention" a bad reputation. For instance, we say the road to hell is paved with good intentions. But intention can be amazing and it can change your life. In my yoga class we incorporate this thinking, to help balance our minds and bodies throughout our session. We stand up and do a balancing pose and everyone is wobbling all over the place. I give the class a minute or so to get adjusted in the pose and hold it for a few breaths. Everyone comes out of the pose laughing and maybe a little frustrated with how off-balance they were. When we explore this more, I find out most of them were focused on falling or not holding the balance just right. We discuss for a moment, what their intention was before moving into the pose.

After our discussion, I direct them to close their eyes and see themselves holding the pose with ease and balance. We visualize this for a few breaths. They open their eyes and I direct them to find a focus in the room and take a breath, seeing themselves in their mind's eye again doing the pose; once they have that intention they can go physically into the pose. The amazing thing is that almost everyone held the pose with ease and steadiness. What they are doing is bringing everything into alignment. They had faith that they would not fall over, but would be balanced and at ease.

Everything in the world except humans follows the will or nature of God. Trees always bloom in spring, their leaves change color in fall and fall off in winter, and then the trees bloom in spring again; this is a continuous process. Nature follows the purpose of its creation. Nature does not question God and His will; it moves with the Spirit that created it and willed it to be. Everything is created with the power of God's intention, and nature is surrendered to that intention. We can disconnect ourselves from this great and amazing power of intention that moves our lives in a direction that will draw us closer to our Creator.

I have seen that intention is aligned with what we believe about something. When we are not connected to the all-creating Spirit, we doubt our lives and our ways get confused. We wonder why we are here and what we are supposed to be doing. Did I marry the wrong person? Will I ever have children or even get married? Will I be successful in my career?

But nature does not ask these questions of God; everything in nature moves with God's intention, so there is no need for these questions. They are doing exactly what God intended, so they are exactly where they should be in life. Yes, we have free will, but I have found that when I use the free will that God gave me to connect with His intention for my life, it flows perfectly. When I depend on the Source, which is God, for all things I need, contentment comes easily.

This is what I believe: God created the universe out of love. When we hold on to this truth, we connect ourselves to God's intention. It is God's intention for me to live a life that is full of love, kindness, beauty, and creativity. God's intention for our lives is to thrive. It is His intention for me to give this to people and to receive this as well. I get disconnected when I try to will things by my own ego and not by the Spirit that wants to lead me to wonderful places.

God has been so gracious to give each one of us the freedom of choice, but this freedom can change your life for the better or for the worse. This freedom has given you the power to assist in molding the world around you. What you put out into the world is what you will get back from this world. It affects everyone, even people you do not know. It affects the spirit of the world.

When you walk in a room and things feel gloomy and negative, you have a choice as to what you will put into that room. Either you will fuel it with the same energy or you will put love, kindness and compassion in that room--and when you make that decision to give love, the Spirit of God will magnify that love. It is contagious, just as hate and negativity are contagious.

When we wonder why negative things are brought into our lives, why we are not doing well spiritually, why there is so much tension in our relationships, we must ask ourselves, "What am I putting out?" What I mean is, when my husband and I are having disagreements, sometimes it has to do with my attitude about him and our relationship. When I am negative and my thoughts are geared toward my husband not changing, I sabotage my relationship. When we have those intentions about something, then this is how it will always be. When we say things like, "I will never lose weight," or "I will never get married," or "I will never—"--then you will never. You are communicating your faith.

In **Matthew 9:29**, Jesus tells a man, **"According to your faith will it be done to you."** In *The Message Bible* it says, "You will become what you believe." It is God's intention for us to thrive, for our lives to be filled with love. He has allowed you to have such a life by your faith and by your connection to the Spirit. However, it is up to you what you fill this faith with.

Be encouraged and fill your faith with good things.

The treasure is not always found at the end of the journey, but along the way.

Lesson 4

Live in the seasons of life

What is your favorite season? I love spring and fall. I love the way the flowers bloom in spring and you see the rebirth of the world after a long cold winter. I also love the fall because of the brilliant colors, the leaves turning red, orange and deep yellow. The crisp air of fall season dancing across my face is so refreshing and all I want to do is curl up with a cup of hot chocolate at my favorite coffeehouse (The Singin Bean). Life is like the seasons and just as seasons pass, so does the moments in our lives. Sometimes, we are in the season of bliss and all is going just as we dreamed. Other times we are in the season of loss and hardship. What we must learn to do in each season is to live in that moment accordingly. We move through the season of life every day. I remember feeling so alone when I was losing many of my family members so close together. I wondered what God was doing in my life. No one close to me was going through what I was facing. No one could relate to me. During this time my oldest son was running away from home and making some very dangerous choices. I was getting sicker with my kidney disease and going from one doctor's appointment to the next. It felt like the world was on my shoulders.

When we face life challenges, we want to ask God why? We want all the drama to pass by quickly or not come at all. Life is not that way. Life is like the seasons. Just because you do not care for the heat of summer, doesn't stop summer from coming. Summer will come. Many times I have lived my life pretending like I was not in the winter of life. I use winter because it is not one of my favorite seasons. Imagine if you will, you dressed and act liked it was summer in the winter. You wore your bikini, shorts and tank top outside, in 20 degree weather. You would go and swim in the ocean and lay out on the beach. You would wear your flip flops in the snow. The truth is you would probably look ridiculous and most likely get very sick. But we can live like this, wishing it was summer instead of winter, wishing it was fall instead of spring. I remember God teaching me a great and simple lesson about this way of thinking. Simply live in the seasons of your life. Surrender to where you are right now. Embrace your pain, just as you embrace your joy.

I remember saying to myself after each funeral I had to attend, after each doctor visit, after each time my son would runaway and come back home, "Lisa this is just the season you are in, this too will pass." When we are in those seasons of life that challenges our very core, take a breath and dress appropriately. Clothe yourself with what is needed at the time. I clothed myself with many prayers. I wrapped myself with compassion and understanding. I secured my heart with God's word and meditation. I nourished my soul with the warmth of great friendships and a loving family. It was not the time to spring out and throw a party and not look at what I was going through. It was my time to find refuge and surrender to this season in my life.

I thank God for all the seasons, even though I have my favorites. Hold on to the fact that each season serves a purpose for the universe and our lives as well.

You are never alone.

Lesson 5

Friendship during the dark clouds

2 Peter 2:23 states, **"When they hurled their insults at him (Jesus), he did not retaliate; when he suffered, he made no threats. Instead he entrusted himself to him who judges justly."**

One of the places I have truly learned about friendships is within the dark clouds of life. During my many years of chronic illness, friends have come in and out of my life. These friends have brought me so much comfort and peace. They have helped me stay close to God and served me in so many ways. To each friend who has touched my life, I say, Thank you. I love the scripture I quoted above because the people Jesus was surrounded by during his last hours on this earth were His friends. But they were going through their own struggles and were not there for Him. When you think about who Jesus could have retaliated against, the first ones that come to mind are the people who persecuted him--the Pharisees (the religious leaders of His time), the crowd hurling the insults, Judas (who betrayed him)--but what about his friends, those who followed Him?

John (the disciple who He loved) deserted Him, as did all the other disciples. Peter (His right-hand man and maybe His best friend) denied him. He could have retaliated against these guys, His closest friends. But instead of reacting with fear, Jesus responded with love and died on the cross for His friends. While He was dying on the cross, He looked down at John and told him to take care of His mother, and after His resurrection He reinstated Peter (to lead the others). I am learning to be like Jesus in my friendships. When you are going through difficult times in your life and the people you care about the most are not there for you, how do you react? I learned in my yoga practice not to react when my body is unable to do a pose, but to respond with love toward myself, breathe through it all, and just relax and let things happen as they are meant to.

How did I take this lesson beyond the mat and apply it to my friendships? When I am facing difficulty in my friendships or any relationships in my life, I need to remember to stop, take a breath, and respond with love and not fear. Deep inside I may be afraid to do this because I want to know what will happen, if my heart will be hurt again, if I will be taken for granted again. Whenever I am like this in my yoga practice, my body doesn't open up; it will not respond well to fear. It is when I just surrender and let go and love myself for where I am and allow that love to project outward that my mind, body and heart open and I experience something real and deeper. This is true with life as well, if I just surrender and respond with love rather than my fear, what is needed is always given freely. Love your friends and be grateful for all kindnesses that are bestowed upon you during your dark clouds. Remember, those you love are somewhere in life themselves trying to do the same thing. God is always there willing and ready to hold your hand through the storm. We are never alone.

Once you live in love you live in truth. It is in this place we stand in the honesty of life and beauty.

Lesson 6

Truth is in Love

"You will know the truth, and the truth will set you free." (John 8:32)

I love this scripture because it communicates HOPE for me. FREEDOM for me. UNLIMITED POSSIBILITIES for me.

But knowing the truth can be a very difficult thing and a long process (especially when living in a lie can be a lot more comfortable).

I remember when I started my pursuit of truth. It was right after my mother passed away. Looking at her lying on the hospital bed lifeless was one of the most honest things I had witnessed in my life. There was no deception of any kind in this moment. She had passed on, no ifs, ands or buts about it. After that moment all I wanted to know was the truth. What is real? What is the truth in my life? Twenty-one days later my grandmother passed away and my search for truth got even deeper, but not until my brother was murdered did everything hit me. TRUTH--I could not be wrapped up in my own lies and fantasies, and definitely not in the ones that the world was feeding me.

So, I started praying for God to lead me to what is true and what is real. He led me to love. Loving God, loving myself and loving others: This is true. This is real. This seems so simple, but I made it my pursuit to love. Some of my friends thought I had lost my mind and was going on some strange pilgrimage. In actuality I *was* going on a spiritual pilgrimage. I started looking at my life and at the ways I was not loving myself, loving God and loving other people. I went to therapy and discovered a lot of truth and got rid of a lot of lies I had lived with for years. I started reading spiritual books and learning how to meditate and listen to the Spirit within me. The Spirit is not called the Spirit of truth for nothing, and it is not a surprise that one fruit of the Spirit is love.

We search for love and truth outside of ourselves, and never think to look within. How do we get to what is true? How do we get to love? Go to the places you try to avoid within yourself and ask yourself, *Why, with a heart of love and compassion? Why* am I compromising? *Why* am I holding on to this bad habit? *Why* am I scared to _____? *Why* do I avoid this person and not confront them about _____? *Why* am I making excuses? *Why* do I come across so hard and not let people in? *Why* do I have to be perfect and always right? One thing I believe is that the answer is behind the *why*. When we allow this one word into our lives and answer with honesty and compassion, we can let go of our personal lies and live in truth. Once you live in love, you live in truth and you are able to change the world around you.

Possess the unseen.

Lesson 7

What is your greatest possession?

In 2002, I lost my mother, my grandmother and my brother. My brother's murder was the hardest for me, following my mom's death. I love my brother very much. When he was small, he used to call me his mama, because I would treat him like my baby doll. Well, when he turned five or six, my treating him like a baby started to get on his nerves, so that ceased pretty fast, but my love for him never has and never will. Losing so many in my family so close together made me feel as though I were losing everything dear to me; my most valuable possession, my family, was fading away. But the truth is, my family is not my possession. They are cherished souls and spirits that God has allowed to love me and touch me as no one else can, but they belong to God. Here is a question I want you to ponder: What is your greatest possession on earth? What is the most powerful thing you hold in your possession? Is it your home, a car, a great portfolio? What about your spouse, children, friendships, or maybe your health?

If these are your greatest possession what happens when you lose one of them or maybe all of them. Do you now possess nothing?

I believe LOVE AND FAITH are my greatest and most powerful possessions. **John 12:1-11** recounts how Jesus brought Lazarus back from the dead. They gave Jesus a dinner in his honor and Lazarus was reclining at the table. People came by to see this amazing miracle. In **verses 9-11**, it says, **"Meanwhile, a large crowd of Jews found out that Jesus was there and came, not only because of him but also to see Lazarus, whom he had raised from the dead. So the chief priests made plans to kill Lazarus as well, for on account of him many of the Jews were going over to Jesus and putting their faith in him."** Because these people put their faith in Jesus Christ when they saw that Lazarus had been raised from the dead, the leaders made plans to take Lazarus' life. They were willing to take a man's life because of jealousy; they would take revenge, because people put their **faith** in Jesus. Satan hates for us to be faithful and he will use anything to take your faith. If you are going through trials, let me reassure you it is not about the situation, it is about your faith.

The Bible says in **1Peter 1:7** that our faith is more valuable than gold. Your faith is your treasured possession. It is the thing that Satan covets from us; he wants your faith. He will use anything against us--our marriages, our friendships, our bodies (health), ours losses, our children, our families, our victories--so that we will lose hope. I think about my brother and my nephew, both of whom were brutally murdered by people they knew, people who allowed hatred, greed, deceit and violence to reign in their hearts. This darkness that people can allow to live inside themselves each day has the potential to take life away. I have learned that I must take this darkness seriously. This is why love and faith are so important. It is crucial that we allow them to reign in our hearts, instead of the darkness (sin).

LOVE is light. This treasure is powerful, because love covers over a multitude of wrongs. Love is infinite. It has no end. It is continuous; if we are giving it out, it will never stop and it is the thing that overcomes the darkness in this world. Love has the power to heal and to change our lives. Love is who God is; **1 John 4:8, "Whoever does not love does not know God, because God is love."**

Remember your great possessions and spread them around with great generosity. You will see a difference in your life. Our faith and our love move mountains not only in our lives, but in the lives of others.

Live in your faith, not your fear.

Lesson 8

Live in your faith not your fears

It can be scary to live in faith, because then you have to do something. Faith without deeds is dead.

I may believe that one day I will be completely healthy, but when I have real faith about it, I will start living like a woman who will be healthy one day. I will eat the way I need to, exercise and start speaking with words of faith and not words of hopelessness. I will fill my faith with good things and not negative things.

Someone told me a long time ago, before I got married, to live like a woman who is going to get married one day. So I learned how to really cook well. I got my house in order. When I went out on dates I treated my date the way I would treat my future husband, with respect, kindness and a serving heart.

Prepare yourself for your blessings. Live in your faith. Believe it or not, you already are living in your faith. Take a look at your life. What has it manifested? Only what you have believed about it. If fear is holding you back from walking in faith that is filled with greatness, do not fret. When you fill your faith with good things, you are walking in your blessing.
If your faith is to be healthy, do not let fear get in the way. You go out and start living a healthy lifestyle. In 2005 I wanted to exhibit my artwork in a gallery, so I started painting seriously and telling others my dreams; in a few months my work was in a gallery. I wanted to get my certification as a yoga teacher. I started taking classes and studying and in a year I got my certification. In 2008, God gave me my health back when my husband donated his kidney to me; after 20 years of chronic kidney disease and months of dialysis, my health was restored. I lived my life as healthy as I could, because I believed God would one day heal me physically.

Whatever your faith is, start living as though it is already so. If you want to be healthier, start eating right and exercising. If you want to get a better job, update your resume, get some new skills, and above all start thanking God for the job you already have instead of complaining. If you want to have great friendships, then be a great friend. And if you want a better marriage, then be a better spouse.

Sometimes we do not live in faith because we are not hoping for great things. Make a list of what you believe. What do you want to see happen? Start with one thing and make a plan of how to live within what you are certain and sure about. Do not let fear grip you and hold you back. Close your eyes and make the leap. You will not regret it.

Beauty has no face.

Lesson 9

A short lesson on beauty

When I was a little girl, my favorite movie was **Mahogany,** starring Diana Ross. I loved this movie. I thought that Ms. Ross was so beautiful and regal. She played an up and coming fashion designer. She made a beautiful life for herself and had lots of beautiful things, but she was so unhappy; all she wanted was to go back to her simple life. Growing up, I cannot say that I felt beautiful as a young woman, even though my mom always told me that I was. I had sandy hair, green eyes and caramel skin, (my legs were skinny as sticks and my dad always told me I was straight up like 6:00, this was not consider beauty in my neighborhood. Consequently, I felt very insecure about my appearance. Thank God I do not have these feelings of insecurity today. Now I may have a bad hair day, but I feel beautiful just the same.

God has taught me what true beauty is and this is the truth I live in each day. This truth has made me feel more beautiful than ever. God's love makes us beautiful! God's love unveils the beauty from which we were formed; we were created with the threads of beauty. To me, everything about God is beautiful, and I was made from that beauty. I was stitched together with beauty. My very essence is beauty. If God used a whisper to create us, it would have been beautiful.

So we are not made beautiful--it is what we *are*, period. I know that I do not always feel beautiful inside or sometimes outside. I have to ask myself what I am connected to. Am I connected to my ego, my looks, and my accomplishments? Will this new dress or these new shoes make me feel beautiful? If my false sense of beauty comes from these sources, then I am connected to ego and not to spirit. These things disconnect us from our Source, (God) and that feeling of being beautiful will fade just as those things fade. My beauty originated from my Source (God). My beauty is not in my physical appearance, but in the beauty of my spirit. When I am teaching yoga, I watch my students, and those who allow themselves to flow with their spirits look so graceful and beautiful, even if the pose is not perfect. It doesn't matter how fit their bodies look; in this moment they are living from the authentic self, and no matter how that is communicated, it is beauty to me and I believe it is beauty to God.

Creation is the vessel, Spirit holds the purpose. When the two are one harmony is born.

Lesson 10

The purpose of the physical

People ask these questions every day: Why I am here? What is my purpose? Now, I will not go into an in-depth discussion of the reason for your existence, but I want to share a lesson I have learned. When life's challenges alter what you think your purpose may be--when you lose your health, your job, a loved one--what happens next?

I have found you really need to understand who you are. If you understand this, your everyday activities change, the people you are around change and you see the world in a different light. When I was in my twenties, I was constantly trying to find out who I was and what I was supposed to be doing with my life. God gave me the answer in my thirties, for now, that is.

Here is the question I had to reflect on: What if you lived in this world through your true identity? I remember when I first start to feel sick from my kidney disease; I felt that my life was over. I lost hope of doing anything really great in my life. I had limitations that would stop me from accomplishing my dreams. A friend asked me one day, "What will you do if this is your life? What will you do if this is the way life will be for you from now on?" That question scared me at first, but over the years God has brought me to my own truth in this.
The lesson He has taught me is this: Our true identities are not in our humanity, but in our spirituality.

God put us in physical form for a purpose and it was not to just live out a human existence. This life is temporary and will pass. So what is the point of Him putting me in a human form in the first place, especially one that is always sick? Dealing with illness for so many years has not been about the physical, but about the spiritual and how God was using my physical form and all my ailments for a divine purpose that has brought Him so much glory and praise.

This is the reason why God put you in physical form. Once you connect with the fact that we are spiritual beings experiencing life in the physical, it will change the decisions you make each day. The truth is your human decisions are affecting the wellness of your very soul. The Source of my soul is where my purpose lies, and

God is my Source. He knows our destiny and why He decided to put us in physical form, and He knows what we are here to do.

I am here to serve God and humanity. I am here to give back what has been given to me. Every moment of my life has a divine purpose; sometimes I see it and sometimes I do not, but God knows it. You do not go to the grocery store just to get groceries when you are living through your true self. We do not go to the mall just to shop, or have the friendships that we have just to fulfill our needs. People do not come into our lives by coincidence. All our actions and relationships are meant for a divine purpose. If you slowed down and just lived through awareness for a moment, you would see it clearly. We are in a spiritual world, hidden by the physical. Just sitting in a meeting and looking at people as spiritual beings makes you see them differently; no matter how they behave, you see them differently, if you look at them with spiritual eyes. Everyone wants to be loved, everyone wants to be treated with kindness, but also everyone wants to love and to be kind. The issue lies with the flesh (the physical); we can be so caught up in the illusions of the world.

The physical is here as a vessel to accomplish the purpose of the spiritual. All that is physical is here to be used for the mission of the spiritual. Everything in your life is a physical manifestation of spirit, and you have the choice of what it will be used for. As I mentioned before, nature understands this. Nature serves God, the universe and humanity, day in and day out. Even though nature is something physical, it understands that it was created by God (the spiritual) and it is surrendered to its purpose.

I do not know what physical vessel God will use to accomplish the spiritual purposes in your life, but be aware that this is why we have the physical. It is here to glorify God in Spirit.

If life is not looking the way you would like, well, you may need to change your prescription. Perception is truly in the eyes of the beholder.

Lesson 11

Getting through the walls

I wrote the following email to my friends when I was told I would have to go on dialysis. It was a very scary time in my life and I was very frustrated as I grew sicker and sicker. Here is the silver lining in this dark cloud of life:

As you know, my health has not being doing well; my kidneys are functioning at 30% and they will put me on dialysis when my function is at 10%, so please pray for God to work His will in this situation.

But I am writing to encourage you. Do you sometimes feel that what you desire or what you are hoping for is on the other side of a huge thick cement wall that you cannot climb over or get around, and the only way to what you desire or what you so desperately hope to receive, you must chisel through the thick cement wall?

Today I cried out to God about my health. As I was praying, I started to scream my prayers and I cried, "God, I feel like I am chiseling through this thick wall and the answer to my prayers is on the other side. My only utensil to get through the wall is a tiny little pick. It is going to take forever and I am just tired. Why is there a wall so thick between me and what my heart desires? Why do I have to chisel at this wall day in and day out?" I felt that this was not fair at all. I just wanted to give up. As I was crying and pondering what I just prayed to God, inside my spirit I heard, "Lisa, there was never a wall between you and your answered prayers, just your perspective of one." Do not get me wrong, I know that our pride can keep us far away from the desires of our hearts, but just give me a moment and look at things a little differently.

My perspective of what is in front of me is what stops me from praying, meditating, doing what is right, persevering through challenging times and even allowing myself to just be happy. When you are having problems in your marriage, what is in front of you? Is it, "He will never change. He doesn't love me anymore. We will never get this right"? When you are having problems with your kids, what is in front of you? Is it, "They just did not turn our right. They will grow up and make the same mistakes I did. They are so selfish and prideful"

When we see a cement wall in front of us, life seems so hard and we feel it will take us forever to get through this wall. And the truth is, when I look at life and my circumstance like that, what takes forever is not how long I have to chisel at the wall, but how long I believe that there is a wall to be chiseled.

We do have challenges to face, but do we have to see them as a wall we must chisel? Why can't the thing that is in front of me just be an opportunity to see God work and see my spirit strengthened? What is in front of me is not a cement wall, but a God who is willing to move me through and over whatever I have to face. When I took on this truth, I did not see a wall anymore, just my God carrying me over my obstacles. The Bible says in **Luke 1:37, "For nothing is impossible with God."**

Nothing is impossible for God and that thick cement wall is just dust in the wind and only needs the breath of my prayers to blow it away.

Do not confuse God with life.

Lesson 12

Who is God in my life?

I wrote this email when I was going through some tough times with my health and started wondering, "Who is God in my life?" Here is what was revealed to me:

Who is God to you? Is God life? Are life and God two different things?
I think sometimes the way I respond to life is parallel to how I see God. What I mean is, when life is going great most of us may think, "God is shining on me and I am doing wonderfully." But when life is challenging we may think, "God is angry with me," or "He has left me alone." Sometimes we confuse who God is with how our lives are going.

I was thinking about my life and wondering, "Why have I felt so tired and run down these past few weeks?" Well, for starters, I am chronically ill, so that happens to me often; on top of that, my whole family, including me, has been sick with some sort of flu, and right after we recovered, I sprained my knee and dislocated my shoulder and hip.

I have been pretty much on bed rest the past few days, but this time with all the rest I feel so tired, a little sad and lonely. I have not felt like eating much and I am not really inspired, so I have been praying for God to inspire me. I want to be in-spirit with you; today I have been resting, reading my books of inspiration and my Bible, but I do not feel inspired.

So, I picked up my husband's old study Bible and just start turning the pages, looking for some inspiration or maybe for an answer to the question I asked God this morning: "Why is it so hard for me to be joyful, upbeat and faithful when life is going as I plan, but it is so easy to be down and feeling sorry for myself when life is not going as I would like?"

I got my answer as I was turning the pages in my husband's study Bible. I started to read a story about a pitcher who found out he had a tumor in his pitching arm and how angry he became with God. I turned the page as soon as I saw what this tale was about. I did not want to read another story about someone sick, but the Spirit moved me to go back and finish reading it. One sentence stood out to me. The pitcher said, "I was confused, I confused God with life."

"Wow, me too," I thought. This is the key for me. Life can blind us to who God really is. God is still the same no matter what happens in my life, good or bad. He is still an all-loving God, an all-knowing God, my protector, my redeemer, my refuge. I am happy to fix my heart and my eyes on who He really is. God saw this morning that my heart was down because I was forgetting who He was in my life and that He is my life, but not the circumstances of my life, good or bad.

The scripture I read this morning was **Psalm 46:10, "Be still and know that I am God."** It does take stillness of heart, mind and sometimes body to just pay attention and know God, plain and simple.

He is not your pains, sufferings and disappointments. He is not the rejection you face in life. He is God, plain and simple. He is not your sicknesses, a hard marriage and difficult relationships. He is God, plain and simple. He is not your victories, triumphs and sunny days. He is God, plain and simple. Get to know who He truly is.

I am not your victories or struggles; I am plain and simple, Lisa. I have an identity and it is not what goes on in your life. With God this is true, and even more. God is not life, and Amen to that. He is my God, plain and simple.

You are the mother of your mind.

Lesson 13

The power of your thoughts

The power of our minds is a subject I have been studying out for years. This study has changed my life radically. I have been moved in my heart and spirit by just being aware of what I allow myself to think each day. The mind is a powerful thing. We have thousands of thoughts in just one day. Our thoughts affect our emotions, our spirits and even our bodies. How we live each day is very much based on what we think about. How we treat others, our husbands, our children and ourselves is based on our thoughts. The same is true of how we communicate with and view God.

We can be caught up and stuck spiritually, and that situation started with a thought. We can have a grudge against someone for days, weeks, months, years and it started with a thought. Where we are in our career, marriage, family and just life, period, started with a thought. So how can we control all these thousands of thoughts we have every day, when we are flooded with so many of them?

What has helped me is meditating and praying. I shared with a friend that when I had my son, my times with God became very challenging. First of all, caring for a newborn while being chronically ill is quite a feat, so I became very discouraged and saw I was pulling away from God, until one day it hit me. What is my relationship with God? Is it this set-up time each day, where I read and pray for a certain amount of time, or is it when I connect with Him? It started with a thought that went something like this: *My relationship with God is going great when I can get up and read and pray for one hour or more every day.* So, what happens when you become chronically ill and have a newborn baby and cannot get up at all? What did this thinking do? It made me feel guilty when I did not do it. It taught me a great lesson, to see that my thoughts are very powerful and I have to take them captive and make them obedient to Christ. Not only do you have to make them obedient, you have to find out the truth within them, because not all of our thoughts are true.

What is my point? Look at what you are thinking, and it can reveal so much valuable insight. In my yoga classes I encourage my students to see that they are the mothers of their minds, because the mind is like a child; it has no direction and can run wild, and our lives will go where we allow our minds to go. Parents we understand this very well, when we allow our children to lead us and control us, by the end of the day we are overwhelmed, frustrated and not having loving thoughts toward our precious little ones. We have to be the ones that lead the flow of the day when we are with our children. Our minds respond the same way. You have to guide it, discipline it and nurture it, or you will be out of control by the end of the day and so will your life. I make my thoughts my prayers, especially my worries. Make that thought of insecurity your prayer. Make that critical thought your prayer; better yet, make it a blessing. Make that fearful thought your prayer. We will have more power over our thoughts when we nurture, guide and discipline our minds by turning our thoughts into prayers to God.

"Do not be anxious about anything, but in everything, by prayer and petition, with thanksgiving, present your requests to God. And the peace of God, which transcends all understanding, will guard your hearts and your minds in Christ Jesus." ~ Philippians 4:6-7

*Each day the universe speaks your worth with a song.
Are you listening to God's serenade?*

Lesson 14

Worthy vs. deserving

I shared the following email when my girlfriends gave me a "Celebrate Lisa's Life" luncheon; this was when I was very ill and I had been in and out of the hospital. I felt so guilty at first about them giving me this party, but God gave me some wonderful insight. Here is the email I wrote and the lesson He taught me within the silver lining:

Good morning! I wanted to share something I learned today that keeps me connected to my Authentic Self versus my ego: Worthy vs. Deserving. I hope you read the first email about Authentic Self vs. Ego Self, so this email will make more sense.

Recently some amazing women in my life threw me a "Celebrate Lisa's Life" party. Just writing about this brings tears to my eyes. I have some incredible women in my life and I pray for everyone to have people like this surrounding you. The ladies surprised me with flowers and gifts and threw the party at this very nice restaurant. I was overwhelmed with gratitude and I am still overwhelmed with gratitude. My friends who could not make it have been sending me gifts and encouragement. When I looked around the table I saw, my best friends, Judith who had organized the event, Julie, Sandy, Sarah, Tami, and Tanisha. These are women that have been in my life through my greatest victories and my greatest challenges. Those that were absent have supported me just as much and I am very grateful for them all.

I am sharing this because the whole time I kept repeating, "I do not deserve this, what have I done? I really do not deserve this!" And the truth is I did not deserve what they did; they lavished me with love. But I was worthy of it. I hope that doesn't sound arrogant, but stay with me for a moment. Here are the definitions for both words.

Worthy- Having worth, merits, or value; useful or valuable

Deserving- to have earned as a right by one's actions; to be worthy of; qualified for or having a claim to reward, assistance, etc., because of one's actions, qualities, or situation

Worthiness doesn't have anything to do with what we have done. It has to do with who God made us and who we are to Him. *Deserving* has to do with having earned something because of what we have done, our actions. I know my girlfriends would say, "Lisa, you have done things to earn this celebration; that is why we threw it." Or maybe not, but I think they would. But any good I have done is from God. Any sacrifice I have made is from God. Any love I have shown is from God. It is God and not me, so I have not earned anything by my actions. Outside of God, to tell the truth, there are some things I have earned and they are not to be celebrated. So why do I say I am worthy of such love? One reason is because God made it so. He communicates it through the universe. "Lisa, you are worthy." Do I deserve it? No, but I am worth it and you are too!

We live our lives sometimes like we are not worth it. We are not worthy of true love, happiness, forgiveness, success, real friendships, or God's blessings, etc.--you fill in the blank. You can see your view of worthiness by just looking at your life. **Genesis 1** is proof that you are worth it. God made us in His image; why? Because we are worth it. God made the universe, the animals, the vegetation, the oceans and sea creatures for us, not for His pleasure; so, why all of this? Because we are worth it. God put Adam in this beautiful garden and when he felt alone, He gave him Eve; why? Not for God's own pleasure, but for us, because we are worth it. And when they sinned against God, and they felt ashamed about their nakedness, He made personal garments for them to cover up (**Genesis 3:21**); why? Because He loved them and they were worth it.

Jesus came to earth and died a brutal death, according to the scriptures, because God and Jesus felt you were worth it. All through the Bible God communicates your worth, and He proves it time after time. But do we live in that truth? I have taken on this truth and my life has been changed because of it. When we know we are worth love, happiness, forgiveness, success, then God's love and blessings will connect you back to your authentic self. You will make decisions that will not compromise this truth. You will start seeing what true happiness and love really are.

When you see your true worth, you will make decisions that will open your life and heart to new possibilities. The word *deserving,* I feel, raises our egos. It is all based on your accomplishments and someone owing you something because of what you did. Ego takes your eyes off how God sees you and put your eyes on what the world owes you. Our focus is on what we deserve. And when we get tired of not getting what we "deserve," we take anything that comes our way. This hurts God's heart because, I believe He looks and says, "You are worth more than that." Remember your worth, live in this place.

Meditation and Affirmation (prayer):

Take a deep breath in as you count to five
Exhale as you count to five
Repeat this affirmation:
"I am worth it, because God made it so. Thank you for this gift."

Repeat this affirmation any time you feel unworthy and you find it hard to receive what God is so happy to give.

Come on in. Life is waiting.

Lesson 15

Come Inside

I wrote this email when I did not want to face my need for a kidney transplant. I wanted to push it under the rug and just pretend I was healthy, but here is one of the things I have learned to live by: **"You must deal with the real, before your soul can be still."**

Do you ever feel that you are disconnected from life? Well, maybe you're living on the outside of life. When we are living on the outside of life, we feel a false sense of security and safety. Here we cannot be hurt, judged, or afraid. But in this place we never truly enjoy the flavors of life. We never truly love the way we really could. We never truly dream as God wants us to dream. We are never truly touched as God desires for us to be.

So look at your life and ask yourself, where is my heart? At work, where is my heart--is it on the inside or the outside? Am I engaged? Am I giving my best? What about my family and friends—am I engaged or disconnected in these relationships? In my marriage, where is my heart--is it on the inside or the outside? Do you feel disconnected from your spouse? Do you feel you do not have anything in common anymore? Well, come inside. Get engaged again with one another.

On the inside, things are alive, life is happening, whether good or challenging. You feel, you hurt, you cry, you laugh, sincere and unguarded. When I was told I was going to have to be on dialysis, I wanted to close my heart and not feel the disappointment or the pain, but when you have to sit in a chair for over three hours, three times a week and allow them to clean your blood, you have to make a choice: Live and feel life, or get really hard and bitter. I chose life and found some of my greatest blessings during this time.

So next time you have the feeling of being disconnected, ask yourself, "Am I on the inside or the outside of life?" Inside of life, inside our hearts, within our challenges and our disappointments we can find some really incredible gifts and live above the surface.

Remember, it doesn't matter how long you have been out there. You can always come in and live.

Sometimes you must journey on the other side of life to experience the beauty of humanity.

Lesson 16

Dialysis—a lesson of life

This email was hard to send to my friends, but it was one of the greatest lessons I shared with those I care so much about:

I wanted to share with you guys some things I have learned being on dialysis. I have been doing my treatments for over a week and God has taught me so much during this short time. I do not know if any of you has ever been in a room with someone getting dialysis treatments, but it is very surreal. During dialysis, you see your blood going out of your body and being cleaned by a machine as a technician monitors you to make sure nothing goes wrong. You are in that room with several other people going through the same treatment. I go to dialysis three times a week and I see the same group of people. We are a family among strangers. I am one of the youngest in the family. My treatments have been very hard on me. They told me the first month is very hard. Sometimes it has been very scary because of allergic reactions I have had to medicines. In it all, God has taught me some amazing lessons.

One lesson God has taught me is that there is a blessing in everything we go through in our lives. When I go to treatment I take a "grateful journal" and I write down what I am thankful for. I say a prayer and send a blessing to all of the people who are undergoing treatment with me. I look into their eyes and smile and just make a human connection saying, "I see you. You are not ignored, overlooked, or put away." I must admit there was a time in my life, even as I have been ill, when I wanted to ignore or not look deeply into people's physical suffering. Yes, I would pray for people and hope they would get better. I would feel bad for each disfigured body, handicap or illness, but I would not want to look any deeper; it was too painful. Going for treatment each time has changed me so much. I see people with missing legs, people with tubes coming out of their necks and arms-- just as I have. I see people being lifted from stretchers onto their dialysis chairs, with the light of life barely in them. I see people crying and moaning. I cannot turn away--they are me and I am them. And God has given me a great opportunity to see myself deeper.

For three hours I sit in a chair watching these people. I see them smile, laugh, tell jokes, talk about their grandchildren and what they did on vacation. And I write in my journal to God that I am grateful for my dialysis, because only here could I experience this side of life. I see people differently. I see life differently. I see suffering differently. I see the humanity and beauty all around me. I see beauty in my friends who have lost their limbs, those with tubes hanging from their bodies. I see beauty, love, compassion, and kindness beyond the physical. I see the spirit of man. So, I am grateful for this place I live in right now. I would not want it to be any other way. Continue to pray for me. I believe God will restore my health. But where I am is all right--now, let me correct this; where I am is *right*. It is my blessing, my gift from God and life.

Forgiveness is the key that unlocks the soul, healing body, mind and spirit.

Lesson 17

Forgiveness

I wrote this email to share a great lesson God taught me about forgiveness. My family went through much turmoil with my oldest son when he was a teen. He was in and out of trouble for six years. His pain brought so much pain to our family, but even with the running away and juvenile detention there were many silver linings. Right now he is getting his life on track and getting into fashion design. (He is really good--but I am his mother, after all.) Here is the silver lining:

How would life be if we lived from a God-centered heart? In my meditation this morning I asked myself a few questions.

> What would life be like if I just lived from the heart, from a God-centered heart?
>
> What would I say today?
>
> What would I do today?
>
> Where would living from such a heart take me?
>
> How would my family be?
> How would my marriage be?
> How would my friendships be?

This silver lining from the lesson of forgiveness came some time later. This morning as I was meditating, the phone rang. I usually do not answer the phone when I am meditating, but something told me to go ahead and answer. It was my son's friend, the friend he has gotten into a lot of trouble with, the friend he recently went to jail with. He wanted to know where Bernard was and if he was still going to church. Reluctantly, I told him how Bernard was doing. I was about to hang up the phone, because inside my heart I felt bitterness and resentment. As I continued to spoke with him, I remembered to live from my heart and not my resentment for this young man, so I asked him how he was doing. He told me how he was doing, and I told him I would let Bernard know he had called, and I hung up.

After I got off the phone, I started to pray for his life and for all the boys my son has hung out with and with whom he has gotten into some very serious trouble. As I prayed, my heart moved me to call him back. Of course, he was surprised to hear back from me. I told him how I felt about the things he and Bernard did that brought our family so much pain, but I also told him that, I was very sorry for being unloving and having bitterness and hatred for him in my heart. There is never any excuse to treat people like this, ever. He was speechless; I told him he didn't need to say anything. He thanked me and we hung up.

After this call I started to cry, because I felt broken in my heart, but I felt connected to this child, just as I am connected to all people. We share the same consciousness with all living beings. I feel Jesus understood this connection. He is the one that made us, all of us. He created the men of God just as He created the tax collectors and He showed love and forgiveness to them all. Jesus lived from a God-centered heart, and in doing this, He changed the world.

For today it changed me, and I believe it changed my son's friend. And I know when my son hears of this from his friend, it will change him.

So today, live from your heart; it may feel scary at first, but it will take you to new places in your life.

Bless

Lesson 18

Blessing others from the silver lining

I wrote this next email when I was going through dialysis every day and trying to find ways to be grateful for all God's blessings. He taught me not only about how He blesses me but about how to bless others. These are the things He revealed to me:

Hi, everyone! I send blessings to all of who receive this email. May your family, marriage, children, work, health, finances, spirit be blessed by God in every way. May this blessing draw your heart closer to God, and may the blessing bring Him glory, honor and praise. I hope this encouraged you without making you feel a little awkward. We do not speak to each other like this on a daily basis, or maybe not at all. My best friend, Julie and I talk to each like this often. We send each other blessings all the time, during our conversations or when we say good-bye. I send blessings to my fellow dialysis patients each time I go for treatment. I send blessings to my neighbors, family and friends.

I started consciously doing this sometime last year when I read an article in a yoga magazine about the power and the obligation we have to bless people. I studied this out, and it is true. We bless, curse or do nothing toward the people that are in our lives. And people are in our lives all the time. In our hearts and with our mouths we either curse them or bless them, or we just let them pass by without a thought. Well, I want to be able to bless the people that come and go in my life each day.

When I studied this out, I was moved. It has made me a happier person within some challenging situations. Now I know we do not think that we curse people, and I bet it is easier to say we do bless people because we pray for things to go great in their lives. Yes, praying for people is sending them blessings. But to understand this a little deeper, I believe it is more than just a hope for something. It is a declaration. It is very important to say it out loud. People in the Bible blessed each other all the time. It was a normal practice. They understood the power of the words they sent out to the people they were blessing.

According to the dictionary, there are several definitions for blessing. Here is one I like: "To request of God the bestowal of divine favor on someone." When you

bless people, is this what you are thinking? Blessing people has made me more conscious, who they are and what they may need. I ask the Lord to bestow health on those that are sick, or sometimes to bestow peace.
But the amazing thing about blessing is that it comes from God.

Here are just a few scriptures about blessing. The verse that sticks out to me is **Luke 6:28**, when Jesus calls His disciples to **"bless those who curse you."** Jesus called them to request that God bestow divine favor on those who curse them. Wow--This is what's convicting about studying out blessing. Blessing those who oppose us is very challenging. It is easier to curse someone who is not treating you right, than to bless them. When people do things you disagree with, like pull out in front of you, or take a parking spot you wanted, or give you a nasty look, or mess up your order (I could go on and on), you know what you say about them under your breath or in your heart. We do not request God to bestow divine favor on them, yet this is what Jesus calls us to do. I believe criticism is just curses, so I have been trying to send blessing instead of criticism in these situations. When I want to be critical of a person, I send them a blessing instead; this has helped my heart and given me compassion for the other person.

So, bless. Call someone today and send that person a blessing. When someone cuts in front of you, send a blessing. When someone gives you a dirty look, send a blessing. Bless your children tonight out loud; let them feel the blessing and hear it from your lips. Bless them, tell them how great they are, who they will be one day. Kids can hear curses all day--let them hear blessings from you. Bless your spouse; we need affirmation from one another. Let's not curse our marriages with words of negativity. Bless your friends. May this practice bless you this week, may it bless your family and friends and all who you come in contact with, and may it bless you as well. Many blessings. I leave you with these wonderful scriptures on blessing:

Genesis 12:3 ~ **"I will bless those who bless you, and whoever curses you I will curse; and all peoples on earth will be blessed through you."**

Genesis 48:9 ~ **"They are the sons God has given me here,"** Joseph said to his father. Then Israel said, **"Bring them to me so I may bless them."**

Exodus 12:32 ~ **"Take your flocks and herds, as you have said, and go. And also bless me."**

Luke 6:28 ~ "Bless those who curse you, pray for those who mistreat you."

Romans 12:14 ~ "Bless those who persecute you; bless and do not curse."

Meditation on Blessing:
Turn off all your phones; sit quietly.
Bring your hands to your heart and inhale deeply and exhale deeply.
Inhale as you count to four and exhale as you count to five (repeat this for two to three minutes).
As you inhale, become aware of the space where your heart is.
Bring your awareness to this space, take another deep inhale and exhale.

Repeat this affirmation:
"My heart is filled with love for all beings. I release all negativity and resentment. It doesn't serve the purpose of my being."

Inhale and exhale and continue to repeat this affirmation for five minutes.
Bring your awareness to someone you need to forgive, see this person in your mind's eye as you inhale and exhale. Repeat this affirmation.
I send blessing to this person. May God bless their lives, their hearts and their souls. May God bring them to a better understanding of who he is and his great love for them.

Pray not only for their heart but pray for yours as well. And if you can, go and make things right with that person.

Just Be.

Lesson 19

Let your being be your service--just be

I wrote this email when I was battling with the matter of how to serve God with my life while being sick most of the time. For many years, I felt so drained that sometimes I did not have the energy to get out of bed. Here is what God gave to me and I passed on to my friends through one of my daily reflective emails:

I wanted to share my meditation and quiet time with you this morning. Of course, this morning I woke up not feeling well. Tyler has been home sick with a bad cold and he just went back to school yesterday. He gave me his little cold. But that's part of being mom.

This morning as I finished doing my yoga I started my meditation. In my meditation I try each day to ask the Lord, "What is it You want me to know today?" And it came to me to read a scripture in Matthew. As I was opening my Bible, it flipped to **2 Chronicles 19:11** ~ **"My sons. do not be negligent now, for the Lord has chosen you to stand before him and serve him, to minister before him and to burn incense.**" As I read this I wondered why God brought this to my attention, so I went on to the scripture that had come to me in meditation, **Matthew 12:17**, which says, **"This was to fulfill what was spoken through the prophet Isaiah: 'Here is my servant whom I have chosen the one I love, in whom I delight.'"**

I know this scripture is talking about Jesus, but I asked God, "Why did You give me these two scriptures?" As I meditated on it some more, He revealed it to me. The common words in each passage are *chosen, to serve*, and *my servant*. God has called me to be a chosen servant, to serve Him for a purpose. Well, when you think of this, you think of the obvious. God has chosen me to do things for him, for others and for His church. But something different came to me.

My illness is my service to God. Sometimes we look at service to the Lord as *doing* things, but I believe that it is also *being*, being something for Him to show the world who He truly is and to give people hope. This is how I have seen my illness as being a service to God. It serves God by showing people God's compassion. It shows people how gracious the Lord can be. My illness shows people how God can work through anyone, no matter what physical, mental or emotional handicaps they may have. It shows how God is my strength. It shows how He cares for the weak and how He makes us strong. My illness serves and confirms the Bible; people look at my life and they see the truth of scriptures like **2 Corinthians 12:7-10, Luke 1:37** and so many more.

What we may be going through in our lives, the trials, the troubles, the disappointments, the pain and suffering--these things could be your service to God. People see you **being** what God calls you to be regardless of the situation, seeing your service to God in this way, and it gives them **hope.** Your service to God in this way can bring glory to God and change so many lives. Look at these moments in your life as a service to God.

Romans 5:3-5 ~ Not only so, but we also rejoice in our sufferings, because we know that suffering produces perseverance, perseverance, character, and character hope. And hope does not disappoint us, because God has poured out his love into our hearts by the Holy Spirit, whom he has given us.

Stay open to life.

Lesson 20

Keep your heart open to life

This email was sent to family and friends when I was hospitalized for the last time before my kidney transplant, and before I was told I had to go on dialysis. This was a very challenging period, because I could feel my body getting weaker and for the first time in a long time I wondered if I would make it through 2008. Here is the email I wrote:

I want to thank everyone who has prayed for me during this difficult time in my life. I want to thank everyone who has made me a meal and taken care of my family. I am forever grateful. Being in the hospital for almost a week and thinking maybe I could die, has taught me a few important lessons that I would like to share with you. So, please bear with me.

First, each day you have a decision to make. Either you will feed your faith or you will feed your fear. When you sit in depression or just decide not to deal with what you're facing, it will not stop your fear from being fed. You will still be feeding either your faith or your fear. They both must eat if they want to survive. As I lay in my hospital bed, I thought about these things. So, even though the doctors came in my room and the nurses checked my vitals and things were not looking better, I had a choice to make, so I would pray and say my positive affirmation, "I am healthy, whole and complete. Thank you, God, for my healing." I would say this as much as I could, no matter how I felt or what the doctors told me. This was a part of me feeding my faith. With our thoughts about our situations, we can feed our faith or we can feed our fears. We can feed both with decisions that we make each day, so each day of my life I wake up and I ask myself, "Lisa, today what will you feed, your faith or your fear?"

The second lesson I learned through all of this is be surrendered to the plan, but not give up my dreams. I believe God has the ability to heal my body, to reverse all that is going on with my health. This is my dream and my prayer. I resisted anything outside of this. My heart was not open to getting a kidney transplant for a while, and I believe that resistance affected my health. My fear was fed more than my faith. I was wondering, "What will happen to me if the kidney doesn't work?"

and thinking, "Oh, I hate taking so much medicine, and I will have to take a lot of medicine for the rest of my life." Getting so sick this last time taught me to surrender to the plan and do what needs to be done—in my case, to stay as healthy as possible and get a new kidney.

The point and lesson here is for me to surrender. I still have kept my dream for God to heal me and reverse this whole thing, and I will believe forever that God has the ability to do this, regardless. The ironic thing is when I went to the doctor's last week, my kidney function had gotten better They were going to put me on dialysis, but my doctor told me that if my kidney function continues to improve, I will not need a kidney transplant. Wow! This is my dream. Sometimes you need to surrender to the plan, and God is gracious enough to give you the dream as well.

The third lesson: Life is not about the condition of your life, but the position of your life. In the hospital I talked to a friend and asked her why she doesn't talk about her dreams. I knew in my heart it was because of fear and the condition of her life. We had a good heart-to-heart talk. I remember telling her what life would be like for me if I lived from a place of condition. I would probably not do anything. I would not become a yoga instructor, due to my health. I would not put my artwork in a gallery or be successful selling my work for a very good price. I would not have come out with my own skin care line. But I did because of my position. My position is this: I am God's daughter. He has put me in place to be great and do great things. He has lined me up with the right people and situations. He has positioned me to do all the amazing things I am doing and have done and will do. It has nothing to do with my condition. I can be in my bed and unable to move and still do amazing things that will draw people to God and move the mountains in my life.

Finally, I have learned do small things to bring about greatness. It is a lesson I have taught to my yoga students. Small changes make big differences. When I got sick, it was the night of the launch party for my skin care line, *B'Tyli Natural Skin Therapies*. I had been sick all week, but the Spirit kept telling me to have this party. Well, after the party my hands and face were suddenly paralyzed and I had to be rushed to the hospital. The doctors thought at first that the paralysis was caused by high potassium levels, but it was not; it may have been a small stroke. To this day they do not know. But whatever the cause, I have not been able to do the things I did prior to that night. Walking and writing have been difficult. Thinking things through has been a challenge. Each day I am getting better, but it has been frustrating. God has taught me to take small steps and be all right with this. When we face difficulties, we like to jump in head first, but then we get overwhelmed and confused. Instead, we need to live in the moment--in the exact moment we are in. No matter what this moment is bringing, live in it and move through it.

So today, I woke up and read, meditated and prayed. I went outside and made a decision that I would walk from my mailbox to my neighbor's mailbox. That felt good, so I went to another mailbox, until I had passed six mailboxes. I did it six times. I felt great and I went in the house and rested. Tomorrow by God's grace I will walk to the stop sign. See, I was frustrated and discouraged because I felt I could not clean my house, cook dinner, take care of my family, do my yoga as I did before. It overwhelmed me as well to think about doing all these things without the energy and coordination I had before all this occurred. I just have to remember that small changes will lead you to big differences in your life and to places of greatness.

These are the things I am learning. I hope they will inspire you in your moments of LIFE. Remember to live in the moment, do what you can right now and let the rest be. Insanity is dwelling on what you do not have right now. Living in the unknown will drive anyone insane. STAY PRESENT.

Update: God blessed me with a kidney transplant, and my husband was my donor. This miracle brought another lesson learned. God's plan is not just for my life, but for the lives of so many people. I wanted just to be healed and knew that would have an impact on many, but this transplant has had an impact on my children, my marriage, my friends and family. It has drawn my heart and spirit closer to my husband; I thought I could not love anyone as deeply as I love him, but my love has grown even deeper. The way God chose to use my husband to heal me has touched and inspired so many people's lives, and every time we tell our story I see others' spirits uplifted. This was truly the perfect plan.

You are the message.

Lesson 21

You are the message

I wrote this email to friends right before my kidney transplant. As I sat in my meditation, I wondered why had I gone through so many trials in my life, and why at this time I was witnessing the suffering of so many of my friends . This is what God gave to me, so I could share it with others:

Something came to me about my life and the lives of those I know who are going through some hardship. You are in a position for people to hear God's voice through you. Maybe you will not have wonderful words of wisdom to bestow on people. But your pain, your hurt, your struggle and how you get through it, could be the very voice of God for those who are witnessing it. One of my greatest lessons this year so far is that **my life is a message**.

I look at myself and the people I know and I see the things we are going through and I think, *Why?* Why are they going through this difficulty at this time in their lives; why that person and not the person next door? Why do they have to feel the pain of loss, why do they have to feel the sadness in their hearts, why do they have to suffer and feel the physical pain? I think about myself and I ask these same questions. And this is what I believe: I am in the position now in my life for people to see and hear God's voice like never before.

If we cling to him, people will see Him through us--through our spiritual, emotional, mental and physical pain and suffering. But what they will see is God's grace, His love, compassion, wisdom, devotion, even God's sense of humor, (yes, God has made me laugh many times during all of this). Do not get me wrong, I do not think you need to suffer in order for people to hear and see God, but suffering can draw us closer to each other. We naturally want to help, to comfort; it makes us stop and pay attention. I know that what I am going through has made people stop and pay attention. I just hope they have seen God more clearly in it all.

So, when you have been put in a position for the world to see God in you, do not regret it or wish it away. Just pray that the world will hear what He has to say. Remember to keep your ears and your heart open as well; the message is also for you. We are the messages; we are living scrolls for all, especially ourselves, to hear and see the voice of God.

Be here now.

Lesson 22

Presence versus perfection

When the dark clouds come, within the silver lining is the lesson that we must not focus on being perfect but on being present in all areas of our lives. I wrote this email when my husband went out of town just a few months after my kidney transplant. It was challenging to have him gone for those two days, but I was physically and emotionally ready to handle him being away. While he was gone, this is what God taught me. Here is the email I sent to my friends; I hope you can find some truth of your own as you read this.

Connection; this word has been on my heart for the past two days. And today I realize why. In the past week my husband has been on a couple of business trips; today he is out of town and next week he is going to a three to four day business trip to Asheville, N.C. He and my son both have been sick with infections and so we all have been off somewhat; maybe this is why I have been thinking about connection.

So many times we can miss out on what is important in our lives because we are focused on what is missing in our lives. We can focus on how things can be better or what we do not have, versus what we do have. I am at my happiest when I am focusing on connecting with the things and people in my life rather than on how perfect or imperfect things are. The ironic thing is that what I am hoping for comes to me, right on time, when I am focusing on connection rather than perfection. But I am at my unhappiest when I am trying to make life perfect, when I am trying to control all that is around me. We look at how our children are not behaving, what they need to improve, but we may miss their hearts, their struggles, their victories, their smiles, hugs and kisses. We can miss their silent cries. We can miss their spirits.

So, sometimes drop the issues and just make conscious efforts to connect with your kids, where they are in their lives, whether it is a good place or not so good. Even in our marriages we can do this. We look at our spouses and think, "You did not do it this way or that way. You forgot to _____; if you would have just _____, then it would have been perfect." Is that really important? What did you miss about your spouse because you were focused on how it could be better? Love what is in front of you and be grateful for what has been given to you at this time.

Now, if this is a struggle for you (and it can be a struggle for me), think about this: If someone is giving you the good they have to give, why is it not enough for you? Why do you need more? Why can you not receive what good they are trying to give? Maybe it is pride, ego, selfishness, or maybe it's something totally different.

This is true in my friendships as well. I learned a hard lesson about friendships many years ago, one which left me with some wisdom. Do not put perfection on any relationship; just connect with the people God has put in your life. Perfectionism can ruin a friendship. In all things be grateful for the gift of that friendship and the blessings it brings, big or small. I have many friendships and I am grateful for them all and for what each one brings. Whatever is given to me, I hope to be thankful always, filled with gratitude that this person thought to give to me, from speaking a kind word to throwing me a fab birthday party.

So I do miss my husband when he goes on a business trip, but I am making an effort to connect with him when he is home. Whether it is one hour in the kitchen making dinner with him or five hours gazing into his eyes, I just need to connect. There was a time in my life that I thought I had been blessed with all my days of being with those I love so dearly and that maybe it was my time to leave this earth and be with God, but He has given me life again. Because of this, I will live each moment, big or small, the expected and the unexpected, to the full. Each day I try to connect with my children, when they are having great days and when their days are not so great. I try to receive with open arms and an open heart what my husband is trying so hard each day to give to me, which is his very heart. I try to receive from my friends whatever they have given, with gratitude. No matter how big or small, even if it is their kind thoughts. Look today for the gift in all things, and connect with those around you.

If things are not going the way you want, throw what you want out the window for a moment and just be present. God seems to always work things out for the greatest good and His glory.

Even in the storms we are blessed.

Lesson 23

Even in the storms we are blessed

One of the most inspiring lessons I learned from living within the silver lining is that I am always surrounded by abundance. I am always being blessed. Even through all my trials, there has always been a blessing. When I could not afford to bury my brother after his murder, a friend on the day of the funeral gave me the money to bury him.

I had so much support around me. When we lost our first baby, a friend told me about an amazing and compassionate doctor who actually had a practice across the street from my house; later he helped me through my high-risk pregnancy and delivered our son Tyler. When I was told I was going on dialysis, God blessed me with a center around the corner from my house; the center had only been open for two years, and the staff was wonderful. They made me feel like I was at home-- being on dialysis for three to four hours at a time, you need to feel as comfortable as possible. And as I have said throughout the book, when I needed a kidney, my donor was the man I had fallen in love with 15 years before. I am always receiving the good in life, despite the dark clouds that come. Here is the email I wrote when I was just meditating on how much I have been blessed:

Here is a quick lesson God taught me this morning.

First, here are a couple of questions that came to mind. Are you served constantly in your life? Do you feel that you are always given to? Think and answer before reading the rest.

If you answered No, think about this. You are in a constant state of receiving. Did you just take a breath? Are you aware of your heart beating? Are you sitting at your job reading this email? Are you at home? Are you thinking of your children, your spouse, your friends? Are you driving your car (hopefully not, if you are reading this email)? Did you get money out the bank or send checks off to pay your bills? Can you think of one person who expressed love to you this week, last week? Can you walk, smell, taste, touch? Did you feel joy, happiness, sadness, encouragement anytime today?

I ask these questions because I thought about this today and it brought me so much gratitude. God is constantly giving to us, all the time. We are always in a state of receiving from His hands, His heart and His spirit. You are always given to, ALWAYS. There is never a time, as long as you have breath in your body that you are not being given to--NEVER. He is always pouring Himself out to us. I know I do not think of these things as I am being given to, but if these things did not happen in my life, I would definitely feel the absence.

I think about marriage and how we do so much for our spouses, things that we all can take for granted. We do so much for our children, things they can take for granted. But we can be this way toward God--breathing, our hearts beating, smelling, touching, yet we can think these things are a given and take them for granted.

The great thing about being ill for so many years is that you know how it feels to possibly lose these *so-called* simple things. When I was very ill, all I wanted to do was touch my children's and my husband's hands. All I wanted to do was smell a coconut cake (it's my favorite flavor). All I wanted to do was laugh with my girlfriends. Dance with my husband without giving out of breath.

Just remember today that you are in a constant state of receiving--so say, "Thank you."

Ability does not rest in the strength or talent of a man, but the connection of his spirit.

Lesson 24

I am able, because He made it so

I wrote this email when I looked back at my life and witnessed all the things I have come through, all the victories I have experienced. It is very good to look back at your life and see where you have come from. It is a beautiful place to be, to have lived and learned in the silver lining of life. It gives you the strength and hope to move through the next dark cloud that will shadow your life. Here is what I shared with my friends and family as I reflected on what God has brought me through. May it help give you strength, hope and courage.

How do we get through hardships and pain?

Philippians 4:13 ~ "I can do everything through him who gives me strength."

Years ago I read this scripture and it gave me so much hope. Here is the definition of each word from this scripture:

Can: to be able to; have the ability, power, or skill to

Do: to perform, to execute, to accomplish, to finish or complete

Everything: all things

Through: from one to another by way of

Give: to deliver in, to place in the hands of, to bestow, to entrust, to guide or direct

Strength: to be strong; mental power, force, vigor, courage, resources, sustenance

Looking at the definitions of these words made this scripture come alive. I looked at the things I have faced in my life and I say to them all: I am able to do this. I am able to go through the death of my family members; I am able to go through the pain of this loss. I am able to get through my son running away, and to face not knowing where he is from day to day. I am able to live my life being chronically ill, living faithfully and with much victory. The beauty and grace of God is that I have done all of this and so much more.

You are able; God has made you able, He has given you the skill, the power, the ability, the know-how. You can perform, execute, accomplish, finish and complete all things. It comes from Him to you. He delivers it to you, He places it in your hands; He bestows and entrusts it to you. He will be the one to guide and direct you. You will have the strength, the mental power, the force and vigor, the courage, the resources and the sustenance to do everything--all things. You can endure the pain you are going through, you can handle the difficulties you are facing. You can be successful and live out the dreams He has given you. Whenever I feel afraid, or feel like I am drowning in life, I remember this scripture, but I also take a check of my own heart.

When we feel we cannot get through something, we have to ask who or what we are we trying to get through this with. If we are trying to go through life on our own power and know-how, if we are trying to get through by relying on our relationships, our spouses or any other means outside of God, then we will not make it through as God has intended us to do. When you just feel stuck and faithless about something, who are you going to for help with your situation? Where is Jesus--is He the path you are walking on? He has to be the one who is taking you through this journey. Our families, friends and spouses are there to help us as well, but they should not be our ultimate SOURCE.

The scripture says I can do everything through HIM; we cannot do everything through human means and human knowledge. We need God. We need Jesus. We need His Holy Spirit. So, be encouraged. You can handle whatever you are facing right now. You have been provided with it all, from His hands to yours. He has entrusted you with the ability, power, skill and know-how. But it must be through Him. Look at your life and say, "I can do this, because He has given me the strength to do so."

Much light and peace to you.

Live in the spaces life has provided.

Lesson 25

Find balance within the space life provides

Most of the lessons I have shared with you are emails I wrote to family and friends. Well, this particular one was not sent out as an email; it is a lesson learned when I had a setback with my kidney transplant. As you know, I received a kidney from my husband (which is such an amazing blessing), but there are risks in any transplant; a lot of transplant patients get a virus called cytomegavirus, or CMV. This virus made me very sick. It affects many organs, especially dehydrating the kidneys and decreasing their function. About seven months after the transplant I started to feel very ill, like I had the flu. My husband had to take me to the doctor and in the office I passed out, so I had to go to the emergency room. I had a very high fever and I had not eaten in days. I was admitted immediately and told I had the CMV virus.

All this was taking place when my husband had just accepted a new job and had to go out of town for training. I was in the hospital so ill I could barely talk or move. Our 8-year-old son was at home with our 22-year-old son, both of them nervously waiting for mom and dad to return home. Dad did, but unfortunately mom had to stay for another five days. I was so lonely in the hospital. My husband did not want to go out of town, but I made him go anyway and his parents came down to take care of our 8-year-old. Each day I just lay in the bed with a fever and the worst stomach pains. I had diarrhea literally every few minutes. For a time I wanted to panic and fret, I wanted to feel faithless, but there was this peace that came over me, no matter what would happen.

During this time I refused visitors, though I have the most amazing friends and family. All I wanted to do is be in the space and find my own balance. I did not want anyone else's input. I knew that people would have given what they felt I needed, but I just wanted to be quiet and hear God. Although I knew that might make people feel strange, this is what my spirit moved me to do. I was so sick; I only had energy for me and God.

I am grateful for all the prayers that were sent my way, all of the love and light helping my body to heal. Each day I got stronger. Each day I learned to surrender, with just me, silence and God. The lesson I learned during this dark cloud was to learn to balance in my own space. I feel that sometimes life brings us into spaces we do not want to be in and instead of finding balance in that space, we just complain and want to be in another space and we do not try to find what we need to get from where we are right now.

When I was in the hospital, I did not come up with this brilliant, spiritual plan. I did not think, "I am now learning to balance in this space." All I knew was that I had to listen to my spirit, to listen to my heart. It was time for silence and healing. I do not regret refusing visitors; it is what I needed to do at the time and I was able to hear God clearly and hear the truth He wanted to give me. I believe that no matter how much I long for my husband to be by my side or to see my little boy's face or my friends' smiles, what needed to happen during those five days happened.

I used the lesson I learned in a yoga class. I told all my students that we would be doing a few poses on blocks today. Everyone's eyes got so large and their mouths opened up with surprise. I smiled at everyone, and told them that this was what I had learned through my five days in the hospital, that you must learn to balance in the space you are in right now. Their expressions taught me a lesson about our human nature. We do not like to be uncomfortable, or to be in spaces we cannot control. We want to know for sure if we can do something or not, before we even try. So I took them through the process with careful instructions, one limb at a time. Everyone was wobbling all over and some even fell off the blocks (the yoga block dimensions are 3x6x9, so you can see they had a very limited space to work with. I let them play with the poses for a while to see how they would learn to balance in the space that was given to them. After a few moments of this, I told each one to come out of the pose gently and start over, but I told them, "You must find your focus, find a place in the room you can focus on while you ease into the pose again." Once they found their focus and kept their gaze on this spot and did not look to the person on the right or the left or even their own bodies, they held those poses on those tiny little blocks with grace and silence. They were surprised that they could balance on such a small base.

This was my lesson gained through suffering with the CMV virus. God taught me to put my focus on Him in silence, to gaze into the eyes of His heart and find my balance in the space that life has provided. Sometimes that space may be a wide-open field or sometimes, as in yoga, it may be an uncomfortable little blue block, but regardless of the spaces you find yourself in, the balance will only come from the place of focus. Let it be on God.

We need the bees for the honey. Life is in balance.

Lesson 26

Life is in balance

After my stay in the hospital, fighting to get rid of the virus that lay dormant in my donated kidney, the day I got out of the hospital was truly a happy day. I was so overjoyed to see my husband and my children. My body had endured so much and I was very weak; just 10 minutes up out of the bed wore me out. My husband was back to taking care of my son and me, working full time on a new job and doing everything around the house. He is such an amazing man and did not complain one time, but he was getting frustrated with this virus. He was not prepared for me to be as sick as I was and for the length of time it took me to get better--as I write this lesson, I am still getting back to health.

When I first came home I focused only on my healing, but a week later I started to feel all the emotions that accompany having been so sick. I had been in this place of well-being for over seven months and I was enjoying it--and then the emotions started to set in. It was great to have my husband and friends to talk to, but one day as I was talking to a friend, she expressed concern (and rightfully so) about how I was doing in my heart, especially with all I had gone through over the past month. I told her, "I don't want to bring my feelings of yesterday back up, but I would be glad to express what God had given me today." As the true and wonderful friend she is, she already knew where my heart lay, and she just listened. Eventually, we did discuss the things my heart had faced; when I was ready to share those hard feelings, she was right there for me. I told her that one of the lessons God has taught me through all of this is that life is in balance. I am learning to look at trials and challenges as the balances of life.

During this time, as I mentioned, my husband had started a new job, as I was dealing with the CMV virus. He was about to go on his first business and training trip to Chicago, while I was lying in a hospital bed. He was blessed with a job that allowed him to stay closer to home, which during my time in the hospital made it convenient for him to pick up our son with no problem, from school. Also, the higher income from his new job provides us with the financial security to take care of all my medicines each month. One of my medicines would cost $3,000 per month, without insurance coverage, and I take about 10 different medicines, including several in that price range.

When I say life is in balance, it really is; we live on the opposite sides of life every day. If it is cold, it will soon be hot and if is hot it will soon be cold. For myself, I would like for all good to come my way all the time. But think about this: All good does come to me in all circumstances, no matter if I am on the hot side of life or the cold side of life.

Here is an email I sent out to my friends and family to encourage them with this lesson I learned within the silver lining:

1. **Life is in balance**, if you open your eyes and heart to see it that way. At the beginning of the year my husband started a new job, which put us in a very comfortable position financially and has given him the challenge he has been looking for in his career--Amen to God's grace. The day after New Year's, I was so sick he had to take me to my doctor and I passed out while he was on the phone accepting the offer for his new job. A week later I was in the hospital with a fever of almost 103 degrees and terribly ill with this virus. But what I learned was that life is in balance; we expect the good times in life all the time, but just as those good times come, so will the not-so-good times. Life is about our growth and drawing near to our God, and that process will, as you will see, come with the good and not-so-good times. I am grateful for the balance of life, which keeps me grounded and humble. It draws me closer to God and others. It defines me, and the person I was created to be shines through, if allowed.

2. **Choose Life until it is not your choice anymore**. The beginning of the year has been very challenging for me and my family, very scary at times. But God has taught me it is my choice how I choose to live through what life brings. It is easy to get discouraged, feel depressed and hopeless, to wonder, "God, what is really going on?" When I had some energy to get up and be about my passions, I found myself just lying there feeling sorry for myself. Living in death, depression, and self-pity is a choice I make, not God. So, until I do not have that choice any more, I choose to live, to live my life to the fullest despite my circumstances. When I was on dialysis and very sick, I would say out loud, "**I choose Life today**, not death, not self-pity, but life."

3. The last lesson came from a friend's statement. I was confessing to her all that I was feeling, the ugly side of my experience and how it has affected me. She told me, "Lisa, look for the beauty in all of this." I told her, "You are right, I need to

look for the beauty, but right now I need to deal with the ugly; **the beauty will come** if my heart is always open to it." I always try to be open to the beauty, to the lessons of my challenges, but you have to be real about the ugly side of things. I asked, "God, what is it you want me to know?"--my favorite, but sometimes very challenging, question I try to ask God often. This is what He told me as I was driving down to Emory this morning: **The beauty will come if you are open to it.** WOW, this is the same thought I had a few days ago!

So please look for the beauty, the blessing in all you are going through, but deal with the ugly as well. If your heart is open to learn what God has to teach you, the beauty will come, and it will help transform you as much as the challenging times.

Rainy days can be beautiful too.

Lesson 27

It is good to be here

This lesson from the silver lining was given to me when my doctors told me that my kidney function was decreasing and I needed a biopsy. I was terrified at the thought of getting a biopsy, and all I wanted to do was to avoid this process. As I have learned, God sometimes has a different plan than what I may want. So, I was at Emory University Hospital being prepped for my biopsy. I had not been there for a few weeks, and it was good to see all the wonderful staff and the familiar faces of other transplant recipients. I was taken to my room, and as I lay on the bed to have my procedure I started to get very nervous. The nurse took my blood pressure and it was very high. She told me she would let me relax and would come back and check it a little later.

As I lay in the bed I crossed my legs in a relaxation yoga pose, *sukhasana* or easy pose. I took in a few deep breaths, relaxed my mind and allowed my body, mind and soul to connect with God. I knew connecting with God would give me the peace and serenity I needed. I could sense the staff looking into my room, wondering what I was doing; one nurse whispered, "She is meditating." I gently smiled with my eyes closed and continued to breathe in and out. A few minutes later the nurse came back to me and checked my blood pressure and it was close to normal. She looked at me and whispered with a smile, "You know what to do." My doctor came in and started the procedure. She was assisted by a new nurse who seemed nervous and did not know where to fit in. She asked me if it was all right for her to stay in the room and assist the doctor. I told her it was. I could see that the other nurses had their own system and she did not feel very welcomed into the clan quite yet. So I started asking her about where she was from (Florida) and how she liked Georgia so far. She was a great comfort to me, and I saw she needed to feel accepted by someone. We connected in a very interesting place, but it was a connection that God gave me during that moment, one that I believe she needed as much as I did.

My procedure and observation time takes about three to four hours, so my dear friend Julie came to visit; she brought me food and sat with me. As I sat in my chair recovering from the procedure, trying to keep still as much as possible, I looked around and observed patients with tubes in their arms.

There were patients who looked very ill because of dialysis. There were others who looked tired and discouraged. One lady sitting a few chairs down from me had skin that was very yellow, which could be a sign that she needed a liver transplant. The truth is, going to my checkups each month is very good for me. I get a chance to see my reality every day, and it moves my heart to be compassionate. It reminds me how wonderful God truly is.

I turned to Julie and said, "It is good to be here." God has brought me to some beautiful moments. When the gift of the silver lining is a moment of spiritual awareness, even when you are in some really dark places in life you will always see the great light within. Many years ago I could not have said those words. All I wanted was for the dark clouds in my life to pass me by quickly or not come at all. But I believe suffering is a blessing within the dark clouds. Sometimes only in our suffering can we see beyond the facades that the ego sets up.

When we are connected to God and our minds are quieted from all the chaos, we can be a part of some amazing moments, no matter what stage these moments are performed on. And our one line can be, "It is good to be here."

Write your story – Now!

Lesson 28

Write your story-NOW!

Several years ago my friends encouraged me to write a book about my life. Well, finally, here I am sitting at my computer and starting to write my first book. It was very painful to write down my life story. It took many attempts, and every time I started I would cry. Remembering the many challenges in my life each day, each month, each year was a bit too much. But I truly did not need to write my whole life story at this time, just some lessons given to me by God from the silver linings of my dark clouds.

When I think of my life, I see victories and I see struggles like everyone else. I see the challenges I experienced growing up in my household with a stepfather who gave me a very hard time emotionally. I see the beauty of my first son's birth, but also the challenges of being a young single mom. I see my wonderful wedding to my amazing husband. I see my second son being born. I see all my beautiful friends surrounding me, who have enriched my life tremendously. I also see many friends who have left my life. I see all my professional victories. I see the two babies my husband and I lost. I see and feel the loss of my mom, grandmother, brother, uncles and great-grandmother within just months of each other. I see my chronic suffering for 20 years--but I also see my husband walking down to my hospital room from his, after he had given me his kidney, to have a date with me.

We can look back at our lives and it can make us happy or it can make us feel sad and disappointed, leaving so many regrets. You must write your story--now. I am not necessarily saying you must sit down at your computer and start to chronicle your life's story (although if the Spirit moves you, go for it). However, I would like to encourage you to start spiritually writing your story; no one else can do this for you. This one is between you and God. I recall someone asking me how I could live my life, with chronic illness everyday and be so happy and positive. Well, the truth is I am not always happy and positive, but I try to write my life story every day. Writing my life story is one of my silver linings. When dark clouds come over my life, I am given choices. I can choose to see the cup as half empty or as half full.

A few years ago I started writing in my journal not how life looked with the human eyes, but how I saw life with my spiritual, faith-filled eyes. Each morning I would get up and sit in my meditation room and look at nature, the sky and trees. I would reflect on God and what He said when He created the earth--**"'Let there be light,' and it was so."** God used His words to bring what He wanted into existence. I looked out from my meditation area and thought, "This bird is here because He said a word that made it so." What amazing power!

Then I thought about the scripture in **Ephesians 3:21 ~ Now to him who is able to do immeasurably more that I could ever ask for or imagine**--He can do more than my wildest dreams. I took a piece of paper and made a list of every area of my life. I thought about each area and I asked myself, "Does this area reflect my wildest dream or even a regular dream?" In some areas I had to say, No.

I began to write my dreams in my journal, telling them to God each day. Here are a few excerpts from that journal:

Marriage--My marriage is filled with love and understanding, passion, respect and truth. My husband is supportive and faithful to me. We are one. It is a holy relationship.
(When I wrote this my husband was facing the fact that he might become a single dad, because my health was deteriorating fast. My last stay in the hospital left me unconscious for three days and doctors did not know if I would make it. God definitely made us one, literally, when he donated his kidney to me.)

My friendships--My friendships are healthy, healing and happy. We take care of each other's hearts.
(When I wrote this I was having some major difficulties in my friendships.)

My health--I am divine health. My body, mind and spirit are always healing and growing. I have all the energy I need to do what is necessary each day. I am healed.
(During this time I was very ill and had been in the hospital twice and had started dialysis.)

My finances--I am a great stewardess of my money. I am disciplined with my finances. I make wise decisions mutually with my husband. Money flows to us easily and abundantly and we use it wisely.
(When I wrote this, there were times money was very tight. Despite it all we were still giving where we could, but in 2008 my husband was blessed with an amazing job, and we have been able to give even more.)

*My oldest son–My son is responsible. He has a great career. He has grown to be a productive man of society. He honors and respects himself and God.
(At that time my son was nowhere near this place and showed no signs that he would be, but today he is doing amazingly well. He is growing and being this creative, productive man, which makes me very proud of him.)*

The most challenging stories I had to write were the ones about my health, my friendships and my oldest son. Each day I would read my story to God. Some days I would feel within my spirit that I was living these things physically (even though they had not manifested in physical form yet) and other days I would just cry because I got news that my health was getting worse. I would see my oldest son in so much emotional pain, but I would still go to my spot and meet with God and read Him my story. I would not give up no matter what. The days I was very sick and could not get out of bed, I would just look at the words and lie back down.

Telling God my story each day was good for me and my faith. We have to speak words of faith over our lives. Whenever you just want something without faith, all you get is want. The Holy Scripture says, **"Faith is being sure of what you hope for and certain of what you do not see."** God wants each of us to have a life that is filled with wonder and amazement.

Jeremiah 29:11 ~ "For I know the plans I have for you," declares the LORD, "plans to prosper you and not to harm you, plans to give you hope and a future."

When you are not writing your story with God and with spiritual, faith-filled eyes, you are letting anyone and anything write the chapters of your life for you. We hear people say, "When I die, I would like someone famous to play me in my life story." Well, when I die I would not mind someone like Halle Berry, Mariah Carey, or Tyra Banks to play me in the Sunday night Movie of the Week, and they can throw a little Angelina Jolie in there for the action scenes. However, until then, take back the pen, get with God and start living the full life He promises. No matter what stage life provides us to perform our story on, let it be the best screenplay ever written and the performance of your life. Bring the house down.

WRITE YOUR STORY--NOW!!

Wear your diamonds today. Life is the special event, and you have an invitation.

Lesson 29

Wear your diamonds every day

Live now. Live today.

I recall my mom getting ready to go out with her girlfriends. I used to sit in the hallway watching her in the bathroom putting on her make-up and fixing the wig she chose for that evening on her head. She would line those perfect lips with a lip pencil and fill it in with her favorite deep burgundy lipstick. My mom's final touch was taking a little liquid liner and darkening the mole next to her mouth. It was her beauty mark; whenever she did this, it always reminded me of Marilyn Monroe for some reason. She would adjust her platform shoes and kiss all her kids good night before leaving. She looked so beautiful. She definitely was a *fashionista*.

The thing I remember about my mother is that she always wore her nice jewelry every day--so did my grandmother and my great-grandmother. They never waited until there was a special occasion to wear their diamonds. They all were divas and loved fashion. Growing up and seeing my mother wear her best jewelry every day taught me a very valuable lesson. We need to wear our diamonds every day.

This may seem very superficial, but not if you knew the women of my family. My mother, grandmother and great-grandmother all were very ill like me. My mom had kidney problems, emphysema and high blood pressure. She was bipolar. In 1999 she found out she had water on her brain and needed surgery. She was in and out the hospital all the time, but she lived her life. Whenever I had to pick her up from the hospital, I would help her put on her clothes. She would say to me, "Lisa, hand me my jewelry." I would watch her put all her nice rings back on her hands.

My grandmother battled breast and colon cancer for 10 years. Even though she had this major illness that was eating away at her body, she looked regal every time I saw her. When she came to my wedding her head was completely bald from chemo, but she put on this peach hat and coordinating dress and she walked with pride down the aisle. The day we buried my mom, my grandmother could barely stand up at the burial site, but she still looked regal and beautiful as always.

My great-grandmother had diabetes and kidney failure, suffering for many years, in and out of hospitals, but she always wore one of the vintage brooches she inherited from her mother. These brooches were so vibrant with color and detail. My great-grandmother's hair had fallen out because of sickness and medications, but you never caught her without one of her fashionable turbans or wigs, never. These ladies traveled the world, went on girlfriend outings, loved life and lived it to the fullest, despite their illness and hardships.

I remember the first piece of Tiffany jewelry my husband bought me. I wore it only for special occasions. I would do the same with all my really nice pieces. When I became really sick and faced the reality that my life could end very soon, I thought, "Why wait for a special occasion to wear my diamonds?" The time to live life to the full is today. When I was on dialysis, before going to the center I would put on my make-up, do my hair and put on a nice casual outfit. The nurses voted me the best- dressed patient in the dialysis center. The choice of going to dialysis was me saying Yes to life, and I was going to feel the best I could feel in this situation. Dressing up for dialysis was not to show off, but to say to the dark clouds of life, "I am living today and I am living to the fullest." Do not wait to live. The dark clouds of illness helped me to see more clearly that life in itself is a special occasion.

So many times in our lives we wait to be happy, to be content, to make the changes in our lives that are necessary for us to reach our goals. We say things like, "When this is right I will be happy, when my circumstances change I will be content." We think that when our spouses change, we will have a better marriage. I remember having fears about the dreams God would put on my heart. I would see only the obstacle in my way, which was my health. I wanted to be a yoga teacher, but the thought that came to mind was, "You are too sick to teach yoga." When I wanted to put my art in a gallery, the thought came to mind, "You are too sick to paint." When I wanted to start my natural skincare line, the thought came to mind, "You are too sick to meet the demands of running a business." Even though I had these thoughts, God's voice spoke louder: Live today. Live now and do not worry about tomorrow. Another way to put it, wear your diamonds today.

I still sometimes fear going after my dreams. When I have these thoughts I go to God and look into that spiritual jewelry box and wear my diamonds with style. I just make the decision to live life anyway. It doesn't matter if I live my dreams for a long time or for a short time. What matters is that I lived them.

WEAR YOUR DIAMONDS TODAY. LIFE IS THE SPECIAL EVENT, AND YOU HAVE AN INVITATION.

Only the soul knows the places you have been.

Lesson 30

Always go back when you can

This may seem like a strange blessing from the silver lining, but it is a blessing to me just the same. When my life is flowing peacefully and things are moving in a beautiful wave, sometimes it is easy to forget my dark clouds, my suffering and the journey on those roads, so I go back to these places and reflect. I call this place my secret garden. I chose this name not because people do not know what is going on in my life, but because I love gardens and only I know the pain, the struggles and the victories my dark clouds have brought to me.

People love gardens for all kinds of reasons. They love to just sit and look at the beauty that surrounds them. They love to hear the sounds of nature, like the crickets, and the birds and the bumblebees. They love to feel the earth beneath their feet. I love gardens for all these reasons as well, but I also love gardens because they slow down the flow of life and help me to really reflect on what life truly is saying to me. I do not like just sitting and thinking about all the hard things that I have faced in my life, but it is good to remember where you have been and where God has lovingly placed you now. It is good to remember the soul-changing lessons He had taught you.

My secret garden does not hold dead trees and leaves, snakes and dry ground. In my secret garden the flowers are brilliant and fragrant, and they represent the lessons I have learned from my challenges. The grass I walk on is luscious and soft to my feet, but at the same time gives me a very secure foundation. This beautiful green grass in my garden represents knowing what God has provided within my spirit, knowing that He leads me to what is true every day for my life. My garden is filled with beautiful butterflies and dragonflies, the true signs of the wonderful transformation God has brought within me. When I enter the gates of my garden I smell the wonderful fragrances of life; when I leave, I am renewed and reminded once again of the spiritual truths that will carry me through this journey of life.

It is good to go back and sit in your secret garden of life and see the beautiful harvest that the silver linings of your dark clouds have brought.

Much peace and light to you always.

I am enough.

Lesson 31

I am Enough

This lesson or you could say, this blessing from the silver lining changed my perspective about what life expects from me. I remember when I was a young girl. I would say things like, "I wish I was the most popular girl in school. "I would wish I was a famous actress, or superstar." I wanted to be everyone except myself. I was never satisfied with who God created me to be.

I was very critical of myself. Nothing seemed to be good enough. When I was a young mom and wife, I felt I could do more. I could have made that meal better or spent more time with my kids. But when my kidney disease started affecting my daily life it changed that way of thinking quickly. I remember making my sons lunch when he was two years old and putting him in the bed with me, because just that one task took all my energy. I told my son, play and eat his lunch while mommy rest. My son, Tyler has grown up seeing his mommy sick. He has seen me in and out of the hospital. He has seen me go through things physically that no child should witness.

My perspective had to change. What was important is just connecting each day with the people I loved. This was enough and what I could give that day was enough.

The feelings of wanting to be someone else left me many years ago. Despite all my sicknesses I love my life and I love who God created me to be. My illnesses and hardships have molded me, by God's artistry, into someone I am happy to be. Sometimes, I do wish my husband married a healthy wife or my boys grew up with a healthy mom, but it is a fleeting thought, because God has taught my family and I, what we have been given in each other is enough. I am enough for my husband and my sons. I am exactly what they need.

God taught me this lesson through my passion. I am a very athletic and strong woman. I taught eight fitness classes a week, during this time my kidneys were failing. When my husband came home from work, homework was done, the house was cleaned and a gourmet meal was on the table. But there was days when none of those things were done and he found me in the bed most of the time, and he had to take me to the emergency room very often. If you allow illness to present its gifts to you, you will find some life changing lessons, in those dark places of life. Being ill taught me, you cannot do it all. Just being is enough. Being here, being present is enough, because many days and months that is all I had to give. This lesson has taught me to live fully and be here now. We miss out so much on life trying to be something or someone we are not. We miss out on the love and passion in our marriage because we want a marriage like someone else. We want kids like someone else. We want to look, dress, etc., like someone else. There is nothing wrong with imitation, I recommend it, but you have to know you are enough. When you see yourself in this way, you are able to move with life and you naturally give of yourself. The insecurities of not being good enough will fade away. When you truly give your heart and move in spirit and truth, you are enough and this is all that is required.

Meditation and Affirmation:
When you are feeling like what you give to this world is not enough.
Sit quietly and take a few breathes. Go through each area of your life in your mind and speak to that area:
Example:
See your marriage and speak to your marriage; say in your mind's eye:
As a spouse I am enough.
As a parent I am enough.

We all have things to work on a change every day. But for a moment give yourself some grace. If you need to change something give it to God and commit to living from a place of love. I want you to remember in God there is balance and truth.

Do what you need to do.

Lesson 32

Do what you need to do

When I was a young woman and faced challenges in my life, my mother would always tell me to do what I need to do and keep it simple. When I think of the phrase, "Every cloud has a silver lining," I always think that it means that every negative situation has something positive in it. I have also learned that sometimes our silver lining is not this mountain-moving lesson or sunshiny blessing. Sometimes your silver lining is you just doing what you need to do, period. Just keep it simple and do one thing at a time. This is how I believed my mother got me through her death.

I remember the day she died. I spent the night at the hospital as usual. I woke up that morning in the waiting room. The strangest feeling came over me. I knew that my mother was going to die that day. She had been in the hospital for a week and the doctors wanted me to make a decision to remove her from life support. This was a very hard decision to make. During my mother's illness, I would go each morning and evening to this huge window in the hospital where I could see the sky and the trees—nature has always made me feel closer to God. That week I asked God to keep my mother alive through February 14th, which is Valentine's Day. I asked him to take her after that day. Well, Valentine's Day passed; it was February 15th and I knew today I would lose Mom.

My friends and family came to visit as usual. My mother's roommate came that evening and brought me a Christmas gift that Mom had bought me, but had not been able to give to me. It was this beautifully wrapped gift box. I could not open it. I knew I had other things to deal with in the next few hours. I thanked my mother's roommate and told her that I was tired, so she left. My husband asked me if I wanted something to eat. I paused before answering him; inside I thought, "I do not need anyone to get me anything to eat, I will not be able to eat, my mom is about to pass on." But I wanted to be alone when this happened, so I told him to go and get me something to eat. He left, and I sat and waited.

A few minutes passed and the lights went off in the waiting room. When the lights went off in the ICU, it meant they were calling the staff to a patient's room because of an emergency. My heart dropped. Everything got quiet inside of me. The doctor came out to the waiting room and called me to the back, to a room called the quiet room, which I passed every day that week and hoped not to enter. I was in the quiet room listening to the doctor tell me, "Your mother is gone." As I sit here and write this, tears flow down my cheeks. I still miss her, but what moves me even now is her whisper, "Do what you need to do, period."

I went outside the quiet room and walked to my window and cried and cried. I thanked God for taking her out of all her suffering. I thanked God for allowing me to have that moment to myself, hearing those words telling me that my mom had died. That was what I needed. I thanked Him for answering my prayer in bringing her out of her unconsciousness to talk to me and giving us that last time with her. Even though she couldn't speak due to the all the tubes in her neck and the tubes in her mouth, she still made us laugh by what she communicated by writing. Her last words to my sister and me were written on an envelope I found in my purse. She wrote, "I love you." I still have the paper.

Planning my mother's funeral was one of the most difficult things I have ever done in my life. I remember going to the funeral home one day and being so exhausted from all the details that I just stopped in the parking lot and could not go on. I could not do this anymore, but I heard my mom's voice, "Lisa, do what you need to do, period." I took a breath and went into the funeral home and planned my mother's funeral, and we buried her a few days later.

This lesson has helped me through some very tough times in my life. It is all right to grieve and be saddened by life. It is all right to feel that something is not fair. It is even all right to get mad. But when the hardships of life come, remember my mother's philosophy: When it is time, "Do what you need to do, period."

Sometimes we get to see the rainbow during the storm.

Lesson 33

Sometimes you can see the rainbow during the storm.

I love rainbows. When I was a kid, I believed the legend of the leprechauns, that there was gold at the end of the rainbow. I remember this really bad storm we had during summer break one year. I had been playing outside, and had to go inside; I sat in my living room, quiet, waiting for the storm to pass. The sky was gray and the rain was pouring down so hard. I thought, W*ell, there goes my day of play*. A few hours later, the rain stopped and the winds died down. To my amazement the sun came out and the sky was blue. I was so happy. I remember running outside with so much excitement. I stood on my patio and looked up at the sky. Wow, there it was: the most beautiful rainbow I had ever seen. The storm was really bad, but it brought the most colorful and vibrant rainbow I had ever witnessed in my life. I have not seen one that vibrant with so much color since.

According to meteorologists, rainbows appear when a dispersion of sunlight goes through raindrops that are still circulating in the atmosphere. This is why we see them once the sun comes out, after a good rain and/or storm. As a kid I loved looking for the rainbows when we had a nice summer rain. I would run outside and look up in the sky, and most of the time I would find my rainbow.

Even as adults we get so excited and mesmerized by rainbows. They are almost magical. I remember when I was in the hospital after my transplant, I had a very bad reaction to some medicine. I was hooked up to so many tubes and monitors. I had about ten hospital staff members around my bed. My chest hurt intensely. The thought going through my mind was, *Am I going to die? My husband sacrificed his life and his kidney for me to live, and now I am going to die and not get a chance to say goodbye to him and my boys.* I started to pray for God to work things out for the best. If it was my time, then it was my time, and I was surrendered to His will. Fortunately, the doctors got my blood pressure and my heart rate back down to normal.

After the ordeal, I sat in my bed that evening looking out my window. My room had two unusual features: a large window from which I could see the beautiful cityscape of Atlanta, and a door that led to a small patio with an iron railing around it. The nurses had told me that the patio was a design idea that looked good on paper, but once built was obviously a liability, so they had sealed the door so no one would get any ideas about. During my six days in Emory University Hospital for my transplant I never saw one bird come and perch on the patio railing. I saw birds fly by my window several times every day, but they never stopped and rested on the patio.

As I lay in my bed, weak from the evening before, I looked out the window and prayed, "God, if I am leaving this hospital alive and well, and I will be restored to health, please let a bird come and rest on my railing." I lay in my bed for hours, and as usual the birds flew by without stopping. I decided to get up and go and pray; I did not want to pray in my room, I wanted to go to the chapel. My friend had been to the chapel earlier that week and had told me how beautiful it was. I asked my nurse if I could please go to the chapel to spend time with God. She paused for a minute, then told me I could go but that I had to put on a yellow gown for protection from germs.

I put on the yellow gown and walked to the elevator, which seemed to take a lifetime. Once I got to the right floor, I slowly walked down the hallway, looking at all the strangers' eyes trying not to stare at me in my yellow gown and hospital socks. I didn't care about the looks; I was alive and grateful to be out of my room. I entered the chapel and went to the prayer book. I read a few prayers and sat down with my head bowed, and I started to pray for the people in the prayer book. Just before I sat up to go back upstairs, a gentle voice said to me, "I prayed for you." It was a lady who had entered the room while I was praying. It touched my heart so much, I started to cry; it was a kiss from God. I went back upstairs and got into bed to get some rest before my evening check-up. Something told me to look out the window. I looked, and there was my bird. I just began to cry. The bird sat perched on my railing for about 30 seconds, but it seemed like 30 days to me. I thanked God for letting me see my prayer answered.

God has answered my prayers in this kind of way many times. I like to think that when He answers my prayers this way, it is His way of allowing me to see the rainbow within the storm. Sometimes we do not have to wait for the storms and the dark clouds to pass us by so we can see the beautiful rainbows in our lives; every now and again, God will let us see the rainbows within the storms.

We sign contracts with life every day. Make sure you are reading the fine print.

Lesson 34

Who are you making agreements with?

I wrote this email when I was listening to negative thoughts, about ever been healed. During this time, I was feeling depressed and discouraged. Here is what was giving to me from the silver lining:

We make agreements every day. What and who you are making agreements with can and will mold and shape your life.

What are you in agreement with, right now? The definition for agreement is this:

1. the act of agreeing or of coming to a mutual arrangement.
2. the state of being in accord.
3. an arrangement that is accepted by all parties to a transaction.
4. a contract or other document delineating such an arrangement.
5. unanimity of opinion; harmony in feeling: agreement among the members of the faculty.

We come into agreements with thoughts, people, and situations all the time. Here is what I mean. Someone may say to you, you are fat, or unorganized, or too slow, or too fast, you name it and when we come into agreement with that person's opinion of us, we will react and respond accordingly. We walk around all day and some of us throughout our lives living with other people's agreements and opinions. Even more convicting is we live with some of our own agreements we have made with ourselves, these agreements can be positive and they can also be very negative. We make agreements such as; my marriage will never change, I will always be sick, I will never lose weight, I will never move up in this company if it depends on these people, this person is out to hurt me, I cannot be trusted, I will never change, etc. We are making these agreements which are shaping our lives and our relationships.

When we take on these thoughts, we are making a pledge and bond with these opinions. Think about this, when we allow ourselves to make agreements with negativity, we are saying YES, to this situation, opinion, thought, etc. We are saying I AGREE WITH THIS!! I agree with the thought, I will never change, my marriage will never change, I am ugly, fat, unsuccessful, etc.

Remember the definition of agreements, to come into mutual arrangements, to be in accord, harmony in feeling.

These agreements we make with life and others will mold and shape our lives, our hearts and characters; it will move you back or move you forward. This revelation has helped me to take captive every thought and make it obedient to Christ.

Satan, always wants me to come into agreement with him that I will not ever be completely healthy and with that agreement I feel sad, depressed, bitter with God and I do feel worst physically, but the other day, I tore that agreement up, even though today I am still not feeling my best. I made another agreement, I agreed with God and his word, I agreed with:
Jeremiah 33:6
'Nevertheless, I will bring health and healing to it; I will heal my people and will let them enjoy abundant peace and security."

God has brought me healing and health, and yes I am human and I will have my times, but I am healed, because God made it so. Today ask yourself, what agreements am I making with life? Are you making agreements with God or with Satan? Are you making agreements with people that are critical of you? Are you making agreements with your faith or your fear? Are you making agreements with your bitterness or your love? Each day with each breath you take you make agreement with life, which molds and shapes not only your day, but your future, as well. Live in harmony with God and all that is pure and true.

Affirmation and Meditation:

Take 5 minutes each day in the morning, right before you start your day to repeat this affirmation. Try to meditate on it as you go about your day when you are choosing what and who you will make agreements with.

I am in agreement with all that is true and pure. I am in agreement with all that will bring the greatest good in my life and in the lives of those around me. I am in agreement with God, and the wisdom of his divinity.

Our silver linings are always with us, even when the storms have passed.

Chapter 35

Your silver lining is always there

I want to dedicate this chapter to the wonderful silver lining God has put in my life. This silver lining is always been there on the cloudy days and the sunny days.

I met my husband, Joseph, in 1993. The first time we ever encountered one another was at a Jack and Jill wedding shower, where I only noticed him for a moment. I really noticed him when I was at the grocery with my roommate and I happen to bump into him and a mutual friend, who introduced him to me. He had the best smile ever, his teeth pearly white and on the side of his cheek a little dimple. I stood still, looking up into his big brown eyes, and said hello and goodbye almost at the same time. This may sound cheesy, but time actually stood still. It was love at first sight.

As I walked away with my roommate, I told her, "I just met my husband." She laughed and told me I was crazy. All I could think about was Joseph. Later on, he told me that he experienced the same thing. We dated for two years and then were engaged for three month before we got married. God blessed me with the love of my life. When we met, I was a single mom with a –six year-old son. Joseph had developed a wonderful friendship with my son even before his relationship with me grew serious; this made me fall in love with him even more. My son was the ring bearer at our wedding. It was a beautiful and memorable day.

Over the years we have faced many victories and many trials. He has been there for me every step of the way. My husband married me knowing I was chronically ill; during our dating relationship there were many days and weeks when I was sick in bed, and he would hang out with my son while I rested.

Like most little girls, I had this dream that my knight in shining armor would come and rescue me from the dragon. Well, I can say my life has had many dragons, and in actuality my husband has been that knight. Before our wedding day, he looked into my eyes and said, "You will always be my princess." As the years have passed he has seen me through many victories and many struggles. He has been my biggest support. When my kidneys failed, he was there at almost every doctor's appointment. And when I was put on the list for a kidney transplant I remember how determined he was to see everything go according to plan. The doctors knew him very well, from all of his following up.

The coolest thing was when he found out he was my perfect match for the kidney transplant. I had seen him this excited only twice, when we got married and when we had our son Tyler. One evening before my transplant he told me, "I prayed to be the one to give you the kidney you needed. I wanted it to be me." I could do nothing but cry. It made me feel that he was my knight in shining armor coming once again to rescue me.

My marriage has not only healed my heart from so many bad relationships I allowed into my life, but it has healed my soul, spirit, and mind—and yes, even my body. My husband is the silver lining that is always with me. We all will have clouds come over our lives and we must, when it is time, live within the silver linings of life's hardships. Here is a beautiful truth God has opened my eyes and heart to: no matter what life brings, my silver linings are always there. Sometimes it just takes a storm to pass for me to see them.

Author's Bio

Lisa Washington was raised in Atlanta, Georgia. She is a kidney transplant survivor. She has been happily married for 14 years to Joseph Washington, Jr., the love of her life and the donor of her kidney. She has two children, Tyler, age 9, and Julian, age 22. Lisa is a certified yoga and meditation practitioner. She is also a self-taught abstract artist who has sold her pieces in the Creative Spirit Gallery in downtown Decatur.

She is the owner and creator of B'Tyli Natural Skin Therapies, an all-natural skin and body care company. She enjoys being with her family and friends. She is currently developing a non-profit organization that will help empower teen moms all over the Atlanta area to believe in the dreams that have already been placed in them. Lisa's new adventure, being an author, rests in your hands today. She hopes that maybe just one experience, one trial she has faced, will bring hope and truth to you.

Authors' Statement:
"May you find truth in all you seek."

Reference List

The Holy Bible, New International Version
Copyright 1973, 1978, 1984 by International Bible Society

THE MESSAGE: The Bible in Contemporary Language
Copyright 2002 by Eugene Peterson. All rights reserved.

NIV/ The Message Parallel Bible. Grand Rapids, Michigan, 49530,U.S.A
Copyright 2004 by The Zondervan Corporation

Resources

Tami Goodwin
Studio Id
President
www.studioidus.com
678-754-3239

Audrey Beauford
Premium Events
404-488-2863

Jennifer Acosta
Jennifer Acosta Photography
www.jacostaphotography.com
email: jacostaphoto@yahoo.com
404-431-2681

Nancy Berry
Certified Editor
Berry1155@charter.net

~NOTES~